G R A P H I S   S T U D E N T   D E S I G N   9 7

GRAPHIS STUDENT DESIGN 97

THE INTERNATIONAL ANNUAL OF DESIGN AND COMMUNICATION BY STUDENTS

DAS INTERNATIONALE JAHRBUCH ÜBER KOMMUNIKATIONSDESIGN VON STUDENTEN

UN RÉPERTOIRE INTERNATIONAL DE PROJETS D'EXPRESSION VISUELLE D'ÉTUDIANTS

EDITED BY • HERAUSGEGEBEN VON • EDITÉ PAR:

B. MARTIN PEDERSEN

PUBLISHER AND CREATIVE DIRECTOR: B. MARTIN PEDERSEN

EDITORS: CLARE HAYDEN, HEINKE JENSSEN

ASSOCIATE EDITOR: PEGGY CHAPMAN

PRODUCTION DIRECTOR: VALERIE MYERS

DESIGNERS: B. MARTIN PEDERSEN, JENNY FRANCIS

GRAPHIS INC.

(OPPOSITE) SCOTT EASLEY

CONTENTS   INHALT   SOMMAIRE

REMARKS   ANMERKUNGEN   ANNOTATIONS

WE EXTEND OUR HEARTFELT THANKS TO CONTRIBUTORS THROUGHOUT THE WORLD WHO HAVE MADE IT POSSIBLE TO PUBLISH A WIDE AND INTERNATIONAL SPECTRUM OF THE BEST WORK IN THIS FIELD.

ENTRY INSTRUCTIONS FOR ALL GRAPHIS BOOKS MAY BE REQUESTED FROM:
GRAPHIS INC.
141 LEXINGTON AVENUE
NEW YORK, NY 10016-8193

UNSER DANK GILT DEN EINSENDERN AUS ALLER WELT, DIE ES UNS DURCH IHRE BEITRÄGE ERMÖGLICHT HABEN, EIN BREITES, INTERNATIONALES SPEKTRUM DER BESTEN ARBEITEN ZU VERÖFFENTLICHEN.

TEILNAHMEBEDINGUNGEN FÜR DIE GRAPHIS-BÜCHER SIND ERHÄLTLICH BEIM:
GRAPHIS INC.
141 LEXINGTON AVENUE
NEW YORK, NY 10016-8193

TOUTE NOTRE RECONNAISSANCE VA AUX DESIGNERS DU MONDE ENTIER DONT LES ENVOIS NOUS ONT PERMIS DE CONSTITUER UN VASTE PANORAMA INTERNATIONAL DES MEILLEURES CRÉATIONS.

LES MODALITÉS D'INSCRIPTION PEUVENT ÊTRE OBTENUES AUPRÈS DE:
GRAPHIS INC.
141 LEXINGTON AVENUE
NEW YORK, NY 10016-8193

■ (OPPOSITE) KEDAR GORE / THE ART INSTITUTE OF ATLANTA
■ (FOLLOWING PAGE) GENNARO CAPASSO / SCHOOL OF VISUAL ARTS

The Harder You Work, the Luckier You Get. BY OLAF LEU

The written articles which appeared in the foreword to the first edition of *Graphis Student Design* certainly are—or rather were—of a general nature. They dealt with questions of what students and their teachers can be, what they should be and what they must be. Neither students nor teachers ever seem to be completely satisfied. But then they never have been. I suppose it all boils down to the old adage: where there's life, there's hope. □ The visual results, on the other hand, paint a different picture. The students' work speaks for itself, and we can only assume that behind their excellent work lies excellent teaching. It just goes to show how limited words can sometimes be. □ *Graphis Student Design* will henceforth set clear new standards for quality in education and training. This is certainly the most important task of the new publication. Great schools you had never known about suddenly jump into the limelight. And schools which had somehow managed to build up a legendary reputation suddenly disappear from the picture. The truth will come out. □ *Graphis Student Design* is setting and will continue to set new standards, creating a new definition of what constitutes excellence in teaching and training. It will force many of those whose work it publishes to turn chance successes into a method of consistently achieving excellence. It's going to be exciting! □ It is not my aim to sing the praises of design training or of design as a profession. Neither do I want to paint a picture of gloom and despondency. What I want is to tell you something about my own country and school, from the point of view of a man who has just turned sixty. I always learned most by studying biographies, being guided by good examples and using them to help me find my own way. □ I am what you might call a no-nonsense practical man. After various temporary teaching posts abroad I finally came to the *Fachhochschule Mainz* (Mainz School of Design) in 1986 when I was fifty years old. Around the age of fifty-five I decided to give up a large and successful practice to devote myself to teaching. My own experience had shown that it is extremely difficult to run a practice and teach at the same time. Young people—students—make demands on your time far beyond the lessons themselves. I have always admired (and sometimes cursed!) those colleagues who have managed to do both at once and who have run up hundreds and thousands of kilometers for the sake of being a professor. As for my choice of school, it had more to do with logistics than with logic: the institute is right on my doorstep. □ I have been at the school of design for more than ten years now. To be perfectly honest, I was at the point of giving up, but so many first-year students have asked me to stay a while longer to see them through their course that I decided to stay. I teach corporate design, a course which combines the study of complex theoretical questions of corporate identity with a completion of realistic project drawn from industry. I would put the mix at about forty percent theory, sixty percent practice. Unfortunately you have to *sell* design too, so I came up with an additional course: "Presentation, Argumentation and Calculation". Since I started teaching it in 1991, this module has become the most popular course our institute offers. Students learn to express themselves properly, to present an argument persuasively and to price their work. It is practical training based on my experience, which complements the theoretical teaching nicely. □ Something else which has been extremely valuable and stimulating are our "practical" events. I called them "Blue Hours" because they originally started late in the afternoon. Well-known designers at the peak of their careers come to talk about their experiences. These events—I arranged twenty-five in all—were soon so over-attended that I decided to replace them with a more low-key version. Thus the "Contact with…" series was born. Again we invite a professional to come and talk, but this time it is only with the class itself. The designer has direct contact with the students, is able to review their work and encourage their professional development. These practical classes often reinforce the things I have already taught the class. □ The *Fachhochschule Mainz* is not so very different from other schools in the area, apart maybe from a few differences in emphasis. We offer book design, for example, which thanks to Gutenberg has a strong tradition in our city. We boast an Institute of Media Design, but this faces stiff competition from Karlsruhe and Cologne. We are also coming up with some good results in illustration. But I wouldn't say that we are by any means a top-ranking school. Just like everywhere else, we have a mixture of students. Since design students do not choose their school based on the reputation of its teachers (although *Graphis Student Design* could do something to change this), good students are a chance occurrence. When good students choose good teachers, it's usually at least partly down to luck (or it was in the past). But I'm firmly convinced that the harder you work, the luckier you get.

Olaf Leu has been teaching corporate identity and design at the Fachhochschule Mainz in Germany for over ten years. He has been a guest lecturer at workshops and seminars around the world. He is Life Member of the Type Directors and the Art Directors Clubs of New York.

Glück auf Dauer hat nur der Strebsame VON OLAF LEU

Die vorwörtlichen Beiträge in der ersten Ausgabe von *Graphis Student Design* sind sicher generalistisch zu nennen: Wie können, sollen, müssen Studenten und ihre Ausbilder sein? Von beiden Seiten ist man nie so ganz zufrieden, ganz nach dem Motto: Solange der Mensch lebt, hofft er. □ Die sichtbaren, weil visuellen Ergebnisse sprechen dagegen eine andere Sprache, zeigen ein anderes Bild: das sehr begabter Studenten, die herausragende Arbeiten vorzuweisen haben – und dahinter darf man die dementsprechenden Ausbilder vermuten. Also ist doch möglich, was verbal immer etwas einschränkend dargestellt wird. □ Die neue Publikation *Graphis Student Design 2* setzt deutlich wahrnehmbare Parameter für Qualität in der Ausbildung – das ist wohl ihr wichtigster und seit langem schon schmerzlich vermisster Aspekt. Plötzlich werden Schulen «sichtbar», die man vorher *so* nicht kannte. Und Schulen, die von einem überholten, aber legendären Ruf leben, werden plötzlich «unsichtbar». Die Wahrheit ist eben eine träge Masse. □ *Graphis Student Design 2* ist und wird Parameter, künftige Rennstrecke qualitativ herausragender Leistungen im schulischen Bereich. Und viele jetzt «Veröffentlichte» werden sich anstrengen müssen, «Zufälle» in «Methode» zu verwandeln. Es wird spannend werden! □ Ich will in diesem Beitrag nicht das Halleluja singen, aber auch nicht das Schreckensszenarium der Ausbildung und des anvisierten Berufes an die Wand malen. Ich will eigentlich als gerade Sechzigjähriger etwas über mein Land und meine Schule erzählen. Ich habe durch das Studium von Biographien immer das meiste gelernt, deshalb ist meine Maxime, an guten Beispielen lernen, sich orientieren. □ Ich bin das, was man einen gestandenen Praktiker nennt. Mit vereinzelter und temporär ausgeübter Lehrerfahrung im Ausland bin ich 1986 im Alter von 50 Jahren an die Fachhochschule Mainz gekommen. □ Im oder ab dem 55. Lebensjahr beschloss ich, die Praxis, ein gut funktionierendes grosses Büro, aufzugeben und mich ganz dem Lehramt zu widmen. Für mich ganz allein hatte ich die Erfahrung gemacht, dass man nur sehr unvollkommen beides machen kann. Junge Menschen, Studenten, fordern Zeit – Zeit über das Unterrichtsmass hinaus. Ich habe Kollegen bewundert (aber auch über sie gelästert), die beides in Einklang brachten und dazu noch viele Transportkilometer von A nach B in Kauf nahmen – nur um Professor zu sein. Meine Entscheidung für die Fachhochschule Mainz war nicht direkt logisch, sondern eher logistisch zu nennen: Sie liegt direkt vor meiner Haustür. □ Inzwischen bin ich über 10 Jahre an diesem Institut

– und eigentlich wollte ich jetzt aufhören. Aber immer sind da noch Studenten der unteren Semester, die mir in den Ohren liegen, «wenigstens sie noch abzuwarten». Und so bin ich noch heute da. Ich unterrichte «Corporate Design», wobei die Theorie über den Identity-Komplex etwa 40 Prozent und die Praxis, d. h. Arbeit an Projekten, die aus der Industrie besorgt werden, etwa 60 Prozent ausmachen. Design muss (leider) auch verkauft werden, also erfand ich ein zusätzliches Studienangebot: Präsentation, Argumentation, Kalkulation. Im Herbst 1991 fing ich damit an – es wurde das beliebteste Fach an unserem Institut. Hier lernt man, sich richtig auszudrücken, zu argumentieren, sich seinem Typ gemäss richtig anzuziehen, man weiss, was man mit seinen Händen tun soll, und man lernt zu kalkulieren. Es ist eine Schule der «Praxis» – meiner Erfahrungen. Somit ergänzen sich beide Programme. □ Äusserst wertvoll und stimulierend zugleich sind die «Praxis»-Veranstaltungen – ich nannte sie, weil sie ursprünglich am späten Nachmittag anfingen, "Blue Hours". Bekannte Persönlichkeiten aus der Praxis plauderten dabei über ihre Erfahrungen. Diese Veranstaltungen, von denen ich genau 25 inszenierte, waren bald so überlaufen, dass ich beschloss, sie durch mehr nach innen gerichtete Veranstaltungen zu ersetzen. So wurde die «Kontakt mit ....»-Serie erfunden. Wieder sind es eingeladene Persönlichkeiten, die im Gespräch, in der Korrektur, im Kontakt mit der Klasse Sichtweisen von draussen nach drinnen übermitteln. Diese Praxisveranstaltungen hatten den Vorteil für mich, dass die Eingeladenen immer das sagten – und somit bestätigten – was ich vorher im Unterricht als Maxime ausgegeben hatte. Es war eine Art Rückkopplungseffekt. □ Mein Institut, die Fachhochschule Mainz, unterscheidet sich nicht wesentlich von im gleichen Raum tätigen anderen Instituten, es sei denn durch einige Schwerpunktangebote wie die Buchgestaltung, die durch Gutenberg in Mainz Tradition hat, das Institut für Mediengestaltung, das aber in harter Konkurrenz zu Karlsruhe und Köln steht, und die Illustration, die gute Ergebnisse hervorbringt. Aber ich würde nie behaupten, wir seien eine herausragende Schule. Wie überall auf dieser Welt gibt es bei uns sehr gute, gute, mittelmässige und mässig begabte Studenten. Weil Design-Studenten ihre Schulen nicht nach der Reputation der dort tätigen Dozenten auswählen (Graphis Student Design könnte das ein klein wenig ändern), sind damit gute Studenten auch Zufallsprodukte. Beide Seiten haben bzw. hatten in der Wahl das berühmte Quentchen Glück. Und Glück hat auf Dauer nur der Strebsame.

Professor Olaf Leu lehrt an der Fachhochschule Mainz «Corporate Design» und «Argumentation, Präsentation, Kalkulation». Er war Gastprofessor bei Vorträgen und Seminaren in aller Welt und ist Life Member des Type Directors Club und Art Directors Club, New York.

Seuls les plus zélés ont de la chance à long terme PAR OLAF LEU

Les préfaces de la première édition de *Graphis Student Design* abordaient un thème que l'on peut qualifier d'ordre général: comment pourraient et devraient être les étudiants et leurs formateurs? D'un côté comme de l'autre, on ne s'est jamais déclaré entièrement satisfait ou, formulé différemment, tant qu'il y a de la vie, il y a de l'espoir. □ Mais si l'on s'arrête sur les résultats visibles, parce que visuels, ceux-ci nous tiennent un autre langage, nous montrent une autre image: celle de travaux d'étudiants exceptionnels, bourrés de talent, qui suggèrent aussi la compétence des enseignants. C'est donc possible, même si, dans les innombrables discussions, on laisse planer le doute. □ Désormais, la publication *Graphis Student Design* établit clairement de nouveaux paramètres de qualité dans la formation – et c'est là que réside sans doute son principal atout, un atout qui a longtemps et cruellement fait défaut. Tout à coup, des écoles méconnues deviennent «visibles» tandis que d'autres, qui vivaient d'une réputation surfaite, deviennent «invisibles». Mais ne dit-on pas que la vérité se cache au fond d'un puits? □ *Graphis Student Design* est et devient paramètre, pose les futurs jalons de la qualité pour les écoles et autres institutions. Et parmi celles dont les travaux ont été publiés, beaucoup devront encore déployer des efforts pour transformer le fruit du «hasard» en méthode. Voilà qui promet d'être passionnant. Mon propos ici n'est pas de noircir le tableau ou de faire les louanges de la formation et de la profession en question. Du haut de mes 60 ans, j'ai l'intention de raconter quelque chose sur mon pays et mon école dans l'espoir que d'autres en feront autant dans les publications à venir. En effet, c'est en étudiant des biographies que j'ai le plus appris, en suivant de bons exemples. □ A vrai dire, je suis ce que l'on appelle un praticien. Après de multiples expériences temporaires faites à l'étranger, c'est en 1986, à l'âge de 50 ans, que je suis entré dans notre institut. Cinq ans plus tard, j'ai décidé de remettre mon cabinet – un grand bureau qui fonctionnait bien – pour me consacrer entièrement à l'enseignement. Je m'étais rendu compte qu'il est impossible de concilier de manière satisfaisante pratique et enseignement. Former des étudiants requiert beaucoup de temps, et le travail ne s'arrête pas à la sortie des cours. J'ai toujours admiré mes collègues (même si je les ai aussi parfois critiqués) qui parvenaient à cumuler ces deux activités, n'hésitant pas à prendre en compte de longs trajets – juste pour être professeur. Le choix de mon école ne reposait pas sur des considérations logiques, mais plutôt logistiques. Elle se trouve à deux pas de chez moi. □ Entre-temps, dix années se sont écoulées depuis que j'enseigne dans cet institut et, en fait, je voulais mettre un terme à ma carrière. Mais il y a là toujours quelques étudiants des premiers semestres qui me glissent à l'oreille: «Attendez encore notre volée!». Et je suis toujours là. Je suis chargé du cours «Corporate Design» qui comprend une partie théorique sur l'identité institutionnelle dans son ensemble et un projet réaliste issu du monde industriel qu'il s'agit de mettre sur pied. Je dirais qu'il y a 40% de théorie et 60% de pratique. Comme le design doit (malheureusement) aussi se vendre, j'ai choisi de proposer un autre cours intitulé «Présentation, Argumentation, Calcul». En automne 1991, j'ai lancé cette nouvelle formule, et c'est devenu le cours préféré des étudiants de notre institut. C'est là que les étudiants apprennent à s'exprimer correctement, à argumenter, à porter les vêtements qui correspondent à leur type, on sait ce qu'il faut faire avec ses mains et on apprend à calculer. C'est une école de la «pratique» – de mes expériences. Les deux volets se complètent parfaitement. □ Tout aussi appréciables et stimulantes, les séances «Pratique» que j'ai surnommées «Blue Hours» parce qu'au début, elles se tenaient en fin d'après-midi. A cette occasion, des personnalités en contact direct avec le monde du travail viennent parler de leurs expériences. Ces séances – à ce jour, 25 au total – étaient si courues que j'ai décidé de les remplacer par une formule plus «intimiste». C'est ainsi qu'est née la série «Contact avec …». Là aussi, les invités sont des personnalités qui amènent des impressions de l'extérieur vers l'intérieur en discutant avec les étudiants, en les corrigeant. Ces cours pratiques ont toujours présenté un avantage pour moi dans la mesure où nos hôtes venaient confirmer ce que j'avais présenté auparavant comme une maxime durant les cours. C'était une sorte de couplage par induction. □ Mon institut – la Fachhochschule de Mayence – ne se différencie guère des autres écoles actives dans le même secteur, sauf peut-être par certains cours proposés, tels que la conception d'un livre qui a une longue tradition à Mayence grâce à Gutenberg, ou par l'Institut de conception des médias fortement concurrencé par Carlsruhe et Cologne. Autre point fort, l'illustration où nous obtenons d'excellents résultats. Pourtant, je n'oserais prétendre ni affirmer que nous sommes une école d'élite. Comme partout dans ce monde, nous avons de très bons étudiants, d'autres qui le sont moins ou qui sont moyens. Comme les étudiants ne choisissent pas leur école de design en fonction de la réputation des professeurs (*Graphis Student Design* peut remédier quelque peu à cet état de chose), les bons étudiants sont en quelque sorte aussi des «produits» du hasard. D'un côté comme de l'autre, la chance a sans doute donné un petit coup de pouce, mais seuls les plus zélés ont de la chance à long terme.

Olaf Leu est chargé des cours «Corporate Design» et «Argumentation, Présentation, Calcul» à la Fachhochschule de Mayence, Allemagne. En tant que professeur invité il a donné des conférences et des séminaires dans le monde entier. Il est Life Member du Type Directors Club et du ADC de New York.

Student Design: Right Place, Right Time? BY STEVEN SKOV HOLT

 Students and professionals alike are now the bene-
ficiaries of a unique moment in time. We are at a
strategic inflection point in that we now exert an
inordinate influence on the future. No matter how
defined, cultural conditions are ideal for an explosion
of new, recently graduated (or not!) design talent. At the same time,
hardware and software developments converge and point toward
entirely new media, manufacturing and self-expressive possibilities. ☐
All of this activity is characteristic of a time when great change is possible. Not only has this turmoil accelerated "infoflow," but it has been
fingered by many cultural critics as a contributing factor in the decline
of literacy in western nations. In particular, the expressions of youth
culture have been singled out and criticized. ☐ I, however, choose to
see abnormality as the new normality and the celebration of our differences as *making* a difference. I see epiphenomena like skateboards,
rap music, post-grunge, hot rods, video games and comic books as
indicators of a new way of being. Beavis & Butthead, Aeon Flux, and
the advertisements and videos of MTV have brought with them the
conditions for a new experiential freedom which we are only now
beginning to tap, understand, and turn back into our design process. ☐
The opportunity is there for a new generation of students to funda-
mentally change the way we see. As the projects found in these pages
show, there can be no more profound task than this (r)evolution of
visual literacy within the context of an emerging ecology of designers'
minds. This new visual literacy is more referential than redundant, more
about scanning than studying, more about designing for change than
designing for constancy. It's already more collaged, cut-and-pasted,
hybrid, juxtaposed, layered, morphed, multivalent, pastiched, speeded
up, super-imposed, twisted, and by turns both more ordered and ran-
dom than any "literacy" before it. ☐ Given this bigger-picture view of our
time's infoflow, creativity, and penchant for change, there is a guarded
sense of optimism in the late 1990s. We're clearly not there yet, but a
sense of possibility pervades the air. Students feel they have to know
more than ever before, and it's true: no generation of design students
has ever faced such high expectations. But from such challenges and
limitations as we now face, unprecedented creative freedoms may be
found. ☐ One problem is that students aren't assigned enough team-
based, interdisciplinary projects. Schools are still producing monolin-
gual graduates who are taught to function primarily as independent
imagists or sculptural isolationists. If the profession were heading in
that direction, that would be fine. But it's not. In my experience, the
really great projects are increasingly about intercultural team creativity, "cooperative competition" and group dynamics. As far as I'm concerned, it's time to collaborate or die.

So, what might design educators, programs, and schools do?

1. Specify a role for themselves within the multiplying universes
of technology. Adopt a point-of-view about the world.

2. Assemble young and old, male and female, black, yellow, red and
white faculty from academia as well as design offices, thereby
bringing real-world "demographic therapy" to the studio experience.

3. Integrate with the larger creative community. Turn the classroom
and campus into a node of professional activity by offering space
and resources for design-aware media, creative non-profit groups,
and local chapters of organizations such as the AIGA and AIA.

4. Publish the results or research of the studio and share it with
other schools so that we know who's doing what, thereby creating
a greater sense of community within the academic community.

5. Offer classes year-round so that students have the option of
moving through quickly or delving more deeply into material
when they need to do so. Get school curricula in sync with the
"24-7-365 society" and the spirit of time-based competition.

6. Offer more internships, in-school breaks, and scholarships for
interdisciplinary work to slow school down when students want.
Give students the curricular flexibility they need so they can step
out, get experience, and build networks during their school years.

7. Proactively establish curricula for degrees in Environmental
Graphics, Interface Design and Information Architecture. Lead
the changes in the profession instead of lagging behind. There
can't be a degree for everything, but programs are urgently
needed in these areas now.

8. Produce graduates for the wide range of career possibilities
that now exist, and will exist in even greater number in the future.
Currently students are trained to become "designers," but there
are many specialties for which they could also be trained: "design
manager," "design researcher," "conceptualist/futurist," "interfacer,"
"design-to-manufacturing expert," "design archivist," and more.

9. Finally, foster innovative ways of looking at or researching the
material culture that we designers produce; it's the end of the
twentieth century, and we have only the dimmest idea about
what we've made, what its effects are, and why we react to certain design elements differently than others.

I look to studies of extreme product or brand loyalty to provide much

*Steven Skov Holt is both strategist for frogdesign, inc., Sunnyvale, California, and chair of the Industrial Design Department
at the California College of Arts and Crafts in San Francisco. He may be reached at 408.734.5800 or stevenh@frogcal.com*

needed perspective. I look to studies of how people customize products to better fit their needs. I foresee a design process informed by the patterns of "Post-Market Product Alteration" that encourages students to create open-ended designs which allow the customer to be the final participant in the design process. □ In ways such as these, I believe we will have not only a revitalized and vastly influential profession, but one that offers students the chance to fervently listen to the user while balancing the often conflicting needs of project brief and self-expression. Our present day concerns with post-credible (near oxymoronic) issues such as industrial ecology, hyperinformation, mass-customization and retro-futurism demand no less. While it's often true that companies such as Frankfurt Balkind, HardWerken, IDEO, Pentagram, Reverb and frogdesign are admired or even idolized by students, I believe that the students in the trenches—sweating the details, inhaling information, and pushing their own (and their classmates') limits by the physical and mental process of "living design" on a minute-by-minute basis—are the real heroes, for they endure the pressures of the past, the challenges of today, and the responsibilities of tomorrow.

Designstudenten: Am richtigen Ort zur richtigen Zeit? VON STEVEN SKOV HOLT

Studenten und Praktiker sind die Nutzniesser eines ganz besonderen Zeitabschnitts. Wir befinden uns an einem strategischen Wendepunkt, an dem wir hier und heute Einfluss auf die Zukunft nehmen können. Wie man es auch immer nennt, die herrschenden wie auch die kommenden kulturellen Bedingungen sind ideal für eine Explosion von neuem Design-Talent, frisch von der Schule (oder auch nicht). Gleichzeitig fliessen gegenwärtig ganze Welten von Hardware und Software zusammen, so dass ganz neue Medien und Möglichkeiten der Herstellung und Selbstdarstellung gegeben sind. □ Diese Aktivität ist typisch für eine Zeit, in der grosse Veränderungen möglich sind. Die rapide Entwicklung hat nicht nur den Info-Fluss beschleunigt, sie wurde von vielen Kritikern auch für den Verlust der Kultur des Lesens und Schreibens in westlichen Ländern verantwortlich gemacht. Dabei wird ganz besonders auf Ausdrucksformen der Jugendkultur angespielt, die mit Umschreibungen wie «unanständig», «aggressiv», «entwürdigend», «zerstörerisch», «verworfen» bedacht wird. □ Ich habe mich zu einer anderen Meinung entschlossen. Ich sehe Abnormalität als neue Normalität. Ich sehe die Zelebrierung der Unterschiede als einen Weg, etwas zu bewirken. Ich sehe in Phänomenen wie Skateboard, Rap, Post-Grunge, Video-Spiele und Comic-Bücher Ausdrucksformen einer neuen Lebensweise. Beavis & Butthead, Aeon Flux und die Werbung und Videos von MTV haben das Umfeld für eine neue Experimentierfreiheit geschaffen, die wir als Designer gerade erst beginnen zu begreifen und in unseren Arbeiten umzusetzen. □ Eine neue Generation von Studenten hat die Möglichkeit, unsere Art der optischen Wahrnehmung von Grund auf zu verändern. Wie ihre Arbeiten zeigen, gibt es keine wichtigere Aufgabe als die (R)Evolution des visuellen Alphabetismus im Kontext eines ökologischen Bewusstseins der Designer. Bei dieser neuen visuellen Lesart geht es eher um Anspielungen als um Ausschmückungen, eher um ein Ausschweifen als um genaues Ergründen, eher um das Gestalten der Veränderung statt um Beständigkeit. Bereits jetzt sind unter den Arbeiten mehr Collagen zu finden, Geschnittenes und Geklebtes, Hybriden - einander gegenübergestellt, überlagert, strukturiert, polyvalent zusammengesetzt, gespeeded, verschlungen und abwechselnd geordnet oder wahllos - als bei jeglicher Darstellungsweise zuvor. □ Mit dieser grosszügigeren Sehweise der neuen Ära der Hyper-Information, in der Kreativität mit einer Tendenz zur Veränderung verbunden ist, lässt sich für die späten neunziger Jahre ein vorsichtiger Optimismus rechtfertigen. Studenten spüren, dass sie mehr als je zuvor wissen müssen, und es stimmt: Keine Generation von Design-Studenten sah sich je so hohen Erwartungen gegenüber. Aber aus diesen aktuellen Herausforderungen und Beschränkungen heraus kann eine unverhoffte kreative Freiheit entstehen. □ Ein gegenwärtiges Problem: Die Studenten sind nicht genügend darauf vorbereitet, im Team oder an interdisziplinären Projekten zu arbeiten. Noch immer produzieren die Schulen Absolventen, die nur eine einzige Sprache sprechen, die gelernt haben, vor allem als unabhängige Bildermacher oder isolierte Bildhauer zu funktionieren. Das wäre in Ordnung, wenn die Branche sich in diese Richtung bewegen würde. Aber sie tut es nicht. Nach meiner Erfahrung geht es bei den wirklich grossartigen Projekten immer häufiger um interkulturelle Team-Kreativität, um «kooperativen Wettbewerb», um Gruppendynamik.

Was könnten also Design-Lehrer/Studienprogramme/Schulen tun bzw. berücksichtigen?

1. Sie sollten in den immer komplexeren Bereichen der Technologie eine eigene Rolle finden, d. h. sich durch einen «Standpunkt» in Bezug auf die Welt definieren, indem sie wirkliches Engagement zeigen.

2. Die Schulen sollten junge und alte, männliche und weibliche

Steven Skov Holt ist Stratege für frogdesign, inc., Sunnyvale, Kalifornien, und lehrt Industrial Design am California College of Arts and Crafts in San Francisco. Er kann unter Tel. 408 734 5800 oder der E-Mail-Adresse stevenh@frocal.com erreicht werden.

Fakultätsmitglieder aller Rassen mit akademischem und mit praktischem Hintergrund engagieren, d. h. den Studierenden sollte eine realitätsnahe, demographische Ausbildung geboten werden.

3. Sie sollten sich in die kreative Gemeinschaft im weiteren Sinne integrieren, d. h. Klassenzimmer und Schule in ein Zentrum professioneller Aktivität verwandeln, indem man designbewussten Medien, kreativen Nonprofit-Gruppen und regionalen Berufsverbänden Raum und Ressourcen bietet.

4. Sie sollten einzelne und/oder Gemeinschaftsarbeiten im Rahmen bestimmter Projekte wenigstens einmal pro Jahr publizieren und an andere Schulen senden, so dass jeder weiss, wer was tut, und ein grösserer Gemeinschaftssinn innerhalb unserer Gemeinschaft entsteht.

5. Sie sollten Studienprogramme über das ganze Jahr anbieten, so dass die Studenten die Möglichkeit haben, das Studium schnell (oder vertieft) abzuschliessen, d. h. ganz im Geiste einer Gesellschaft ohne Zeit und des Zeitdrucks in der Praxis.

6. Sie sollten Praktikantenstellen vermitteln und Stipendien für interdisziplinäre Arbeit vergeben, so dass die Studenten das Studium unterbrechen können, um Erfahrungen zu sammeln und Verbindungen noch während des Studiums aufzubauen.

7. Sie sollten Studiengänge anbieten in den Bereichen Umweltgraphik, Gestaltung von Benutzeroberflächen und Darstellung von Informationen.

8. Sie sollten Studenten für das grosse Spektrum der heute vorhandenen Möglichkeiten ausbilden sowie für das noch grössere zukünftige Spektrum. Heute werden die Studenten zu Graphikern/Designern ausgebildet, aber es gibt viele Fachrichtungen, für die man sie auch ausbilden könnte: «Design-Manager», «Design-Forscher», «Konzeptualist/Futurist», «Gestalter von Benutzeroberflächen», «Experte für die Herstellung vom Entwurf bis zur Produktion» etc.

9. Und schliesslich sollten sich die Schulen zur Förderung innovativer Wege entschliessen, die der Betrachtung und Erforschung der materiellen Kultur, die wir Designer produzieren, dienen; wir befinden uns am Ende des 20. Jahrhunderts und haben nicht die leiseste Vorstellung dessen, was wir gemacht und bewirkt haben, und wir wissen nicht, warum wir auf bestimmte Design-Elemente mehr reagieren als auf andere.

Ich befasse mich mit Studien extremer Produkt- oder Marken-Loyalität, und ich befasse mich mit Studien über die Art, wie Leute im wirklichen Leben Produkte verändern, um sie ihren Bedürfnissen anzupassen. Und diese Verhaltensweise wird zukünftige Studenten dazu ermutigen, "Open End"-Designs zu entwickeln, so dass der Verbraucher zum letzten Glied in der Design-Kette wird. □ Wenn wir in der hier beschriebenen Richtung fortfahren, werden wir meiner Meinung nach eine Branche wiederbelebt haben, die nicht nur grosse Auswirkungen hat, sondern auch den Studenten die Möglichkeit gibt, aufmerksam auf den Verbraucher zu hören und gleichzeitig eine Balance zwischen Auftrag und Selbstausdruck zu finden. Während Firmen wie Frankfurt Balkind, HardWerken, IDEO, Pentagram, Reverb und frogdesign heute von vielen Studenten bewundert, wenn nicht gar ideologisiert werden, finde ich, dass die Studenten selbst die wahren Helden sind. Sie müssen den Druck der Vergangenheit, die Herausforderungen der Gegenwart und die Verantwortung für die Zukunft tragen.

Etudiants en design: au bon endroit, au bon moment? PAR STEVEN SKOV HOLT

Etudiants et professionnels bénéficient en ce moment d'opportunités uniques. Nous nous trouvons en effet à un tournant stratégique qui nous permet d'exercer en même temps une influence immense sur l'avenir. Parallèlement, nos univers de hardware et de software ont commencé à converger, annonçant l'émergence de tout nouveaux médias et de possibilités fantastiques tant pour l'industrie qu'en termes de créativité personnelle. □ Toute cette activité en fusion et en ébullition est caractéristique d'une époque où de grands changements sont possibles. Cette évolution galopante qui a contribué à accélérer le flux d'informations est jugée par les critiques culturels comme un facteur responsable de l'apparition du phénomène d'inculturation dans les pays occidentaux. Les formes d'expression de la culture des jeunes sont ainsi mises au pilori et jugées «inappropriées», «choquantes», «dégradantes», «dangereuses» et «corrompues». □ Je préfère opter pour un autre point de vue. Je considère l'anormalité comme la nouvelle normalité. La célébration des différences est un moyen d'avancer. Pour moi, les épiphénomènes comme le skate-board, le rap, le post-grunge, les jeux vidéo et les BD sont plus les indicateurs d'un nouveau mode de vie. Beavis & Butthead, Aeon Flux ou encore les pubs et les clips de MTV ont ouvert la voie d'une nouvelle liberté expérimentale que les designers commencent seulement à découvrir, à comprendre et à intégrer dans leur travail. □ La nouvelle génération d'étudiants a

Stratège de l'agence frogdesign, inc., Sunnyvale, Californie, Steven Skov Holt est aussi directeur du département de design industriel au California College of Arts and Crafts (CCAC) de San Francisco, Californie. Tel. 408 734 5800. E-Mail: stevenh@frocal.com.

ainsi la chance unique de changer radicalement notre façon de voir les choses. Comme en témoignent leurs travaux, il ne peut y avoir de tâche plus importante que cette (r)évolution de la culture visuelle liée à une nouvelle conscience écologique du designer. Cette nouvelle culture visuelle est plus référentielle que redondante, elle s'attache plus à scanner qu'à étudier et s'inscrit davantage en faveur du changement que de la constance. Hybride, polyvalente, speedée, tordue dans tous les sens, elle privilégie les collages, les coupé-collé, les juxtapositions et les pastiches, et est tour à tour plus ordonnée et plus aléatoire que toute autre «culture» précédente. □ Au vu de cette nouvelle ère d'hyperinformation où la créativité s'accompagne d'un certain goût du changement, on peut faire preuve d'un optimisme prudent pour la fin des années 90. Les étudiants sentent qu'ils doivent en savoir plus que jamais, et c'est vrai: aucune génération d'étudiants en design n'a été confrontée à des exigences aussi élevées. Néanmoins, les défis et les limites auxquels nous devons faire face ouvrent aussi la voie à une liberté créative sans précédent. □ Un problème actuel est que les étudiants ne participent pas assez à des projets interdisciplinaires, basés sur un travail en équipe. Les écoles continuent à produire des diplômés monolingues auxquels on apprend à fonctionner uniquement comme créateurs d'images indépendants ou sculpteurs isolés. Si la profession évoluait dans ce sens, cela ne poserait pas de problème. Mais ce n'est pas le cas. Selon mon expérience, les projets vraiment intéressants requièrent de plus en plus la créativité d'équipes pluriculturelles, une forme de «compétition créative» et la dynamique de groupe.

Que pourraient faire ou prendre en compte les professeurs, les programmes d'études et les écoles?

1. Préciser leur rôle au sein des univers complexes de la technologie, c.-à-d. se définir par rapport au monde en faisant preuve d'un engagement réel.

2. Réunir jeunes et anciens, hommes et femmes de toutes races, issus aussi bien du milieu universitaire que d'agences de design, c.-à-d. offrir aux étudiants une thérapie démographique internationale axée sur le monde réel.

3. Encourager l'intégration à la communauté créative, c.-à-d. faire des classes et des campus un carrefour de l'activité professionnelle en encourageant les médias s'occupant de design, les groupes créatifs sans but lucratif et les organisations professionnelles locales en leur fournissant les moyens nécessaires.

4. Publier au moins une fois par an les résultats de travaux individuels et/ou collectifs, les envoyer aux autres écoles afin que chacun sache qui fait quoi et contribuer ainsi à renforcer le sens de la communauté au sein de notre communauté.

5. Proposer des cursus toute l'année afin que les étudiants puissent achever rapidement (ou approfondir) un cycle, c.-à-d. leur offrir des programmes d'études adaptés au monde du travail où le facteur temps est déterminant.

6. Proposer plus de stages, d'interruptions et de bourses pour les travaux interdisciplinaires afin de rallonger la durée des études en fonction des besoins des étudiants, c.-à-d. leur offrir un enseignement suffisamment souple qui leur permette de sortir de l'école, d'acquérir de l'expérience et de tisser des relations durant leurs années d'études.

7. Prendre les devants en créant des programmes d'études en graphisme environnemental, en création d'interface et en architecture des informations, c.-à-d. anticiper les changements dans notre branche plutôt que de se laisser dépasser par les événements.

8. Former des diplômés à même de répondre aux multiples offres d'emploi du marché qui seront de plus en plus nombreuses à l'avenir. Les étudiants d'aujourd'hui sont formés pour devenir graphiste ou designer, mais ils pourraient se spécialiser dans bien d'autres domaines: «design manager», «chercheur en design», «conceptualiste/futuriste», «créateur d'interfaces», «expert de la fabrication du projet à la production», «archiviste graphique» pour ne citer que ces exemples…

9. Enfin, encourager les façons novatrices de regarder et d'étudier la culture matérielle que nous, designers, produisons. Le XXe siècle touche à sa fin, et nous n'avons qu'une idée très vague de ce que nous avons fait, des effets produits par notre travail, et pourquoi nous réagissons plus à certains éléments de design qu'à d'autres.

Je me suis penché sur des études consacrées à la fidélité des consommateurs à un produit ou à une marque. J'ai également examiné des études visant à établir dans quelle mesure les consommateurs personnalisent certains produits afin de mieux les adapter à leurs besoins. Je pense que les futurs étudiants créeront un jour des designs «open-end» qui feront du consommateur le dernier maillon de la chaîne. □ Si nous poursuivons dans cette voie, je suis convaincu que nous réussirons à revitaliser notre branche dont l'influence est immense. Les étudiants pourront ainsi être véritablement à l'écoute des consommateurs tout en conciliant les impératifs du projet et le besoin d'affirmer leur talent créatif.

Irreverence as Form. An Advertising Experiment. BY JEFFREY METZNER

It became clear to me a few years ago that the generation of 15-25-year-olds resented being advertised to, that their fingers were firmly placed on the "bullshit buzzer"—especially if they smelled a big corporation trying to talk to them in their own language. Did a twenty-year-old junior in college really need to be told to "Be young, have fun, drink Pepsi"? □ The question for me was, how can advertisers like American Express, Proctor & Gamble, Prudential Insurance etc. reach this massive group of potential consumers? After studying magazines thick with advertising created by and for this new generation for companies with names like *Transworld Snowboarding & Skateboarding*, *Warp*, *Thrasher*, *Big Brother*, *Grand Royal*, *Paper*, *Electronic Gameplayer*, *RayGun*, *Wired* and for networks like MTV, VH1, and ESPN2, I began to get a picture of how these young people are talking to each other. They are breaking all the rules, including sacred and practical ones which dictate the need for readability and continuity. □ As a young art director at Doyle, Dane, Bernbach, I was brought up on Mr. Bernbach's rules of advertising which all boiled down to "The Idea Is King." For better or for worse, advertising has followed this path for the past thirty years. Advertising agencies worldwide have borrowed from the Bernbach philosophy and most of what is called "good" advertising reflects this past. □ This new generation, however, looks at all this as "the old school," and with no mercy is writing its own rules, borrowing from pop culture to communicate with each other. The work is irreverent, ironic, spontaneous, and because of the computer technology, executionally driven. This generation hasn't thrown out the need for the big idea; it just recognizes that it doesn't stand alone. □ I thought it was important to address these evolutionary changes with a group of seniors at The School of Visual Arts in New York who are working to build their portfolios in order to get good jobs. At the end of the year, we had a show at the Art Directors Club of New York. I was surprised and relieved by the positive reaction from the advertising community and the media to the work of my students. I had been working in the dark for two semesters hoping that the approach that I was so sure of wasn't a figment of my already too-active imagination. I was in fact commandeering a senior advertising portfolio class to break as many rules as possible, to be irreverent, ironic, outrageous, possibly a little dirty and maybe even rude. I wasn't interested in moral or sexual irreverence; we've all been seeing too much of that for a long time. I was encouraging social rebellion. □ As I look at the work of these students, I take so much pleasure in the humor, the irony, and the irreverence to false gods: gods of typography, beauty, continuity, readability and—the highest god of all—the God of False Sincerity. I really get a kick out of so much of this work—it forces me to think about myself and to question my motives in spending so much of my energy causing each one of these pieces to happen. □ The tone of this student work is really that of my story. In much of my own work and my own life I have always managed to create a fair amount of friction. At times I've gone way out of my way to surprise, to reveal, to question or to deflate the pretentious. I always understood that friction causes energy. I am well aware that the general nature of the energy and philosophy of the class is subversive. Bob Dylan hit it perfect for me when he said, "If my thought dreams could be seen, they'd probably put my head in a guillotine. (But it's alright Ma, it's Life and life only)." □ I have always had a rebellious nature, but as I've gotten older I have learned to revere certain things which I have come to consider "sacred." □ Because of the success of last year's class (all these students found good jobs right away), it is exciting and relevant for me to continue to follow this path. I confess—it's true that the big idea isn't the only thing on my mind. My search is for a balance between execution and idea and I believe it is definitely possible for execution to lead. □ I insist that the advertising speak in the voice of the generation that it is trying to reach. I always ask my students to try to break through the "code" of the deeply-embedded, cherished, subconscious "rules." The overriding emotions of these students are courage and fear, the latter being the most common. I take enormous pleasure in watching students slowly overcome fear and not let it stop them from becoming themselves. □ The real value of this class is not so much in the work as it is in the process of trying to speak in an original voice. Although I stand by *all* the work, I also recognize the difficulties involved in selling work this extreme in the real world. We must remember we are trying to reach a select audience. I think it's important to have a good balance of this "alternative" work and more classic forms of advertising in order to have a great portfolio. □ At the end of the day, if there is anything that I wish I could give these students it is the understanding that anything goes and there are no rules...except the golden ones.

Jeffrey Metzner is a freelance graphic designer, art director, creative director and painter. His many awards for creative excellence include Clio and Andy awards and a Gold Medal from the Art Directors Club. He is a professor in the Media Arts department at the School of Visual Arts in New York.

Pietätlosigkeit als Formprinzip, ein Werbeexperiment VON JEFFREY METZNER

Vor ein paar Jahren wurde mir klar, dass die Generation der 15 bis 25 jährigen Werbung nicht ausstehen kann, besonders wenn sie nach Anbiederung riecht, d. h. wenn ein grosses Unternehmen versucht, sich ihrer Sprache zu bedienen. Musste man einem einundzwanzigjährigen College-Studenten wirklich sagen, dass er «jung sein, Spass haben und Pepsi trinken» soll? ☐ Ich stellte mir deshalb die Frage, auf welche Art Firmen wie American Express, Proctor & Gamble, Prudential Insurance etc. diese riesige Gruppe potentieller Konsumenten erreichen könnten? Ich sah mir Zeitschriften mit viel Werbung an, die von der neuen Generation für die neue Generation gemacht wurde, und zwar für Firmen wie Transworld Snowboarding & Skateboarding, Warp, Thrasher, Big Brother, Grand Royal, Paper, Electronic Gameplayer, RayGun, Wired, und für Sender wie MTV, VH1 und ESPN2. Dabei bekam ich allmählich eine Vorstellung davon, wie diese jungen Leute miteinander reden. Sie brechen sämtliche Regeln, einschliesslich unumstössliche und praktische, die Lesbarkeit und Kontinuität predigen. ☐ Als junger Art Director bei Doyle, Dane, Bernbach wurde ich ganz im Sinne von Mr. Bernbachs Prinzipien der Werbung erzogen, die alle auf folgendes Credo hinauslaufen: «Was zählt, ist die Idee.» Die Werbung hat diesen Leitsatz in den letzten 30 Jahren schlecht und recht befolgt. Werbeagenturen in der ganzen Welt haben Anleihen bei der Bernbach-Philosophie gemacht, und das meiste dessen, was als gute Werbung bezeichnet wird, reflektiert dieses Erbe. ☐ Für die neue Generation jedoch ist das die «alte Schule», und um miteinander zu kommunizieren, stellt sie gnadenlos ihre eigenen Regeln mit Anleihen bei der Pop-Kultur auf. Die Arbeiten sind respektlos, ironisch, spontan und Computer-Technologie dominiert die Ausführung. Diese Generation bestreitet die Notwendigkeit einer grossartigen Idee nicht; es geht nur nicht mehr allein darum. ☐ Ich fand es wichtig, diese evolutionären Veränderungen mit einer Gruppe älterer Studenten an der School of Visual Arts in New York aufzunehmen. Sie sind dabei, ihre Arbeitsmappen zusammenzustellen, um sich zu bewerben. Am Ende des Jahres hatten wir eine Ausstellung beim Art Directors Club von New York. Die positive Reaktion der Werber und Medien auf die Arbeiten meiner Studenten hat mich überrascht und auch erleichtert. Ich hatte quasi zwei Semester lang im Dunkeln gearbeitet in der Hoffnung, dass meine Auffassung, von der ich so überzeugt war, nicht vielleicht das Ergebnis meiner bereits zu lebhaften Phantasie sei. Ich hatte einer Werbeklasse des letzten Semesters empfohlen, möglichst viele Regeln zu brechen, respektlos, ironisch, unverschämt und möglichst ein bisschen schmutzig oder vielleicht sogar anstössig zu sein. Es ging mir nicht um moralische oder sexuelle Respektlosigkeit, davon haben wir schon genug gesehen. Wozu ich ermuntern wollte, war eine soziale Rebellion. ☐ Wenn ich mir die Arbeiten dieser Studenten ansehe, freue ich mich über den Humor, die Ironie und die Respektlosigkeit falschen Göttern gegenüber: dem Gott der Typographie, der Schönheit, der Kontinuität, der Lesbarkeit und – dem höchsten von allen – dem Gott der falschen Aufrichtigkeit. Viele dieser Arbeiten bereiten mir riesiges Vergnügen. ☐ Der Ton dieser Studentenarbeiten entspricht meiner eigenen Geschichte. Es ist mir gelungen, in vielen meiner Arbeiten und in meinem Leben für ein angemessenes Mass an Reibungen zu sorgen. Manchmal bin ich weit über mich hinausgegangen, um zu überraschen, aufzuzeigen, Anmassendes in Frage zu stellen bzw. vom Sockel zu holen. Mir war immer klar, dass Reibung Energie erzeugt. Und ich weiss genau, dass die allgemeine Natur der Energie und Atmosphäre in der Klasse subversiv ist. Bob Dylan hat es auf den Punkt gebracht: «In meinen Gedanken sind Träume, die mich sicher den Kopf gekostet hätten. (Aber es ist o.k. Ma', es ist das Leben und nichts als das Leben)». ☐ Ich bin von Natur aus rebellisch, aber mit steigendem Alter habe ich gelernt, bestimmte Dinge zu respektieren, die mir inzwischen «heilig» geworden sind. ☐ Der Erfolg der Abschlussklasse des letzten Jahres (alle Studenten fanden sofort gute Jobs) ist ermutigend. Ich suche nach Ausgewogenheit zwischen Ausführung und Idee, und ich bin überzeugt, dass auch die Ausführung das Wichtigste sein kann. ☐ In Werbung muss die Sprache der Generation sprechen, die sie erreichen möchte. Von meinen Studenten erwarte ich, dass sie den Code der liebgewonnenen «Regeln» im Unterbewusstsein knacken. Die Gefühle dieser Studenten schwanken zwischen Mut und Ängstlichkeit, wobei letztere dominiert. Es macht mir grosse Freude zu beobachten, wie die Studenten diese Ängstlichkeit langsam überwinden und zu einer eigenen Sprache finden. ☐ Der wahre Wert dieses Studienganges liegt nicht so sehr in der Arbeit wie im Entwicklungsprozess, der zu einer eigenständigen Persönlichkeit führt. Obgleich ich zu all den Arbeiten stehe, bin ich mir doch bewusst, wie schwer es ist, so extreme Arbeiten in der Praxis zu verkaufen. Wir dürfen nicht vergessen, dass wir versuchen, ein bestimmtes Publikum zu erreichen. Ich glaube, es ist wichtig, eine gute Mischung dieser alternativen und der klassischen Form der Werbung zu haben, um eine wirklich gute Arbeitsmappe vorzeigen zu können. ☐ Was ich den Studenten vermitteln möchte, ist das Bewusstsein, dass alles erlaubt ist und dass es keine Regeln gibt....ausser den goldenen.

Jeffrey Metzner ist freier Graphiker, Creative Director und Kunstmaler. Er arbeitet ausserdem als Professor an der Fakultät Media Arts der School of Visual Arts. Zu den vielen Auszeichnungen, die er für seine Arbeiten erhielt, gehören der 'Clio', der 'Andy' und eine Goldmedaille des New York Art Directors Club.

L'irrévérence comme forme. Une expérience publicitaire PAR JEFFREY METZNER

Il y a quelques années, je me suis rendu compte que la génération des 15-25 ans détestait la publicité qui s'adressait à elle, en particulier lorsqu'une importante société essayait d'adopter un langage «branché». Un lycéen devait-il vraiment s'entendre dire «Sois jeune, amuse-toi, bois Pepsi»? □ La question qui se posait alors pour moi était de savoir par quels moyens des firmes comme American Express, Proctor & Gamble, Prudential Insurance, etc., pouvaient atteindre ce large groupe de consommateurs potentiels? Après avoir passé au crible d'innombrables magazines regorgeant de publicités créées par et pour cette génération pour le compte de sociétés comme Transworld Snowboarding & Skateboarding, Warp, Thrasher, Big Brother, Grand Royal, Paper, Electronic Gameplayer, RayGun, Wired et pour des chaînes comme MTV, VH1 et ESPN2, je commençai à mieux cerner la façon qu'ont les jeunes de communiquer entre eux. Ils transgressent toutes les règles établies, font fi des sacro-saints préceptes et autres critères pratiques prévalant au besoin de lisibilité et de continuité. □ En tant que jeune directeur artistique chez Doyle, Dane, Bernbach, j'ai été formé aux règles publicitaires édictées par Monsieur Bernbach qui toutes partaient du principe que ce qui compte, c'est l'idée. Ces trente dernières années, la publicité a suivi cette devise à la lettre pour le meilleur et pour le pire. Les agences de publicité du monde entier ont adopté la philosophie de Bernbach, et beaucoup de ce que l'on considère comme une «bonne» publicité reflète le passé. □ Pourtant, la nouvelle génération voit là la vieille école et établit, sans pitié aucune, ses propre règles, s'inspirant de la culture pop pour communiquer. Les productions sont irrévérencieuses, ironiques, spontanées et largement influencées par la technologie informatique dans leur exécution. Cependant, cette génération n'a pas renoncé à la recherche de l'idée maîtresse, simplement d'autres paramètres entrent en ligne de compte. □ J'ai pensé qu'il était important de s'attaquer à cette évolution avec un groupe d'étudiants plus âgés de la School of Visual Arts de New York occupés alors à constituer des portfolios afin de décrocher des postes intéressants. A la fin de l'année, nous avons présenté le travail accompli à l'Art Directors Club de New York. Je fus à la fois surpris et soulagé de constater la réaction positive des professionnels de la publicité et des médias. Durant deux semestres, j'ai travaillé à l'aveuglette espérant que l'approche que je préconisais n'était pas une pure création de mon imagination déjà par trop débridée. En fait, j'avais demandé au groupe chargé de réaliser ces portfolios publicitaires de transgresser un maximum de règles, d'être irrévérencieux, ironique, outrageant et, si possible d'avoir l'esprit un peu mal tourné, si ce n'est d'être inconvenant. Il ne s'agissait pourtant pas de briser des tabous d'ordre sexuel ou moral – de ce pain-là, nous n'en avions déjà que trop mangé –, mais d'encourager les étudiants à une rébellion sociale. □ Lorsque je regarde les travaux de ces étudiants, je me réjouis de l'humour, de l'ironie et du manque de respect témoignés envers de faux dieux: le dieu Typographie, celui de la Beauté, de la Continuité, de la Lisibilité et – dieu parmi les dieux – celui de la Fausse Sincérité. Ces productions sont une véritable stimulation. □ Le ton de ces travaux traduit ma propre histoire. Dans bon nombre de mes réalisations comme dans ma vie, je suis toujours parvenu à créer des frictions. Parfois, je suis sorti des sentiers battus pour surprendre, révéler, remettre en question ou faire tomber tout ce qui me paraissait prétentieux. Pour moi, il a toujours été clair que toute friction est productrice d'énergie. Et je sais très bien que la nature générale de l'énergie et de la philosophie de la classe est subversive. Bob Dylan l'a très bien exprimé: «Dans ma pensée, il y a des rêves qui auraient sans doute valu à ma tête d'être guillotinée. (Mais c'est bien ainsi Ma', c'est la vie, et rien que la vie).» Je suis rebelle de nature, néanmoins, les années passant, j'ai appris à respecter certaines choses qui, entre-temps, sont devenues «sacrées» pour moi. □ Le succès rencontré par la classe terminale de l'année passée (tous les étudiants ont tout de suite trouvé de bons jobs) m'encourage à poursuivre dans cette voie. Je reconnais que trouver l'idée maîtresse n'est pas ma seule préoccupation. Je recherche un certain équilibre entre exécution et idée et suis fermement convaincu que l'exécution peut primer sur tout le reste. □ Selon moi, la publicité doit parler le langage de la génération qu'elle vise. De mes étudiants, j'attends qu'ils transgressent le «code» des règles les plus chères à leurs yeux, lesquelles sont profondément ancrées dans leur subconscient. Devant la tâche exigée, les étudiants entretiennent des sentiment mitigés: ils sont partagés entre courage et crainte, mais c'est cette dernière qui l'emporte, même si je constate avec plaisir qu'ils surmontent peu à peu ce sentiment pour devenir eux-mêmes, se trouver. □ La véritable valeur de cette classe ne réside pas tant dans le travail que dans le processus évolutif qui débouche sur une personnalité propre. Bien que tous les travaux recueillent mon approbation, je sais combien il est difficile de vendre des travaux aussi extrêmes dans la pratique. Il ne faut pas oublier que nous essayons d'atteindre un public cible bien précis. Je pense qu'un bon portfolio publicitaire doit contenir à la fois des productions alternatives et d'autres, plus classiques. □ Ce que j'aimerais que les étudiants comprennent, c'est que tout est permis et qu'il n'y a pas de règles... excepté les règles d'or.

Jeffrey Metzner est professeur au département Media Arts de la School of Visual Arts. Il travaille également en tant que designer graphique indépendant, directeur de la création et peintre. Ses nombreuses distinctions comprennent les prix Clio et Andy ainsi que la médaille d'or de l'Art Directors Club.

STUDENT

DESIGN

NINETY-SEVEN

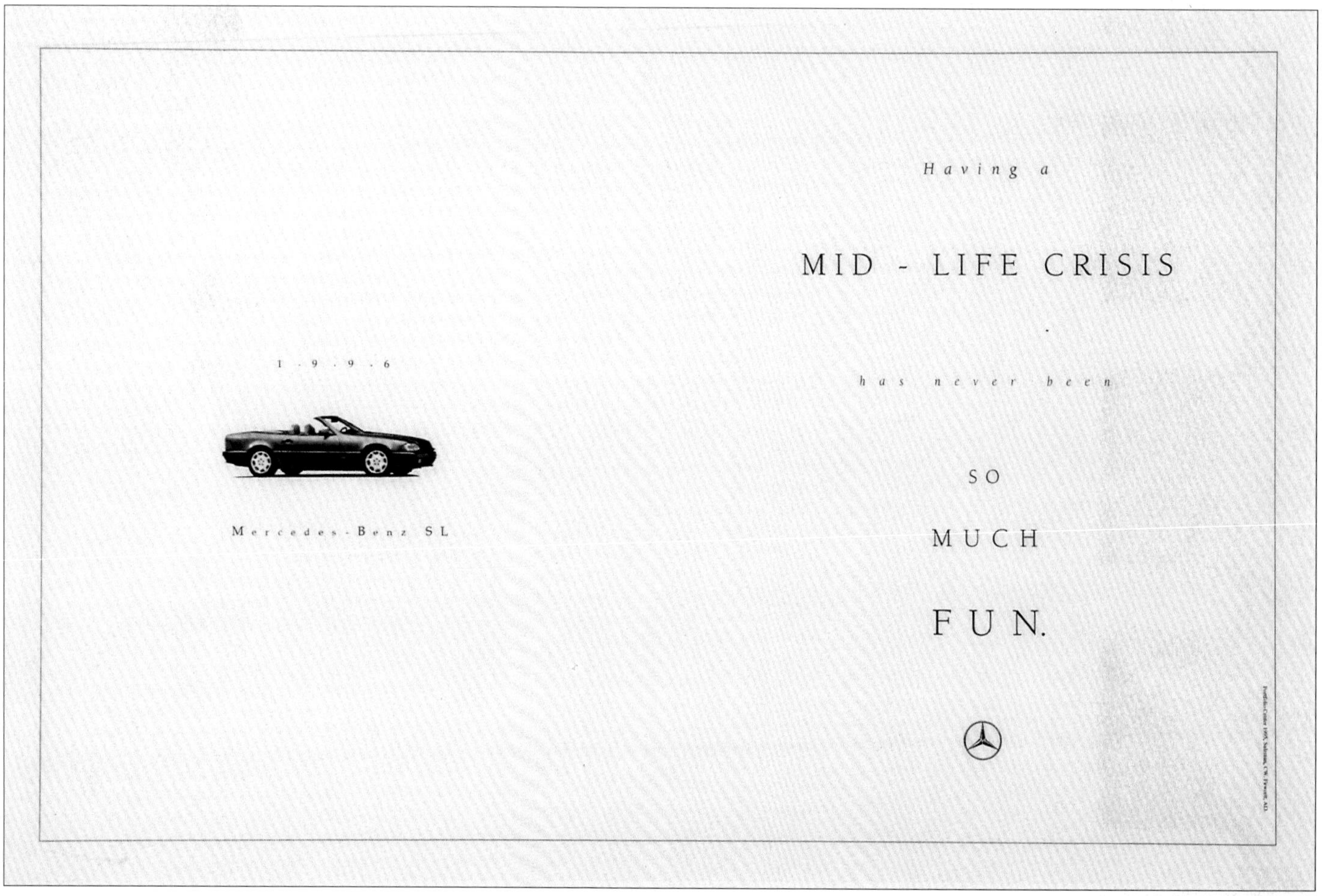

Having a

MID - LIFE CRISIS

·

has never been

SO

MUCH

FUN.

1 · 9 · 9 · 6

Mercedes·Benz SL

Cheaper than

MARRYING

a woman

HALF YOUR

AGE.

1 · 9 · 9 · 6

Mercedes·Benz SL

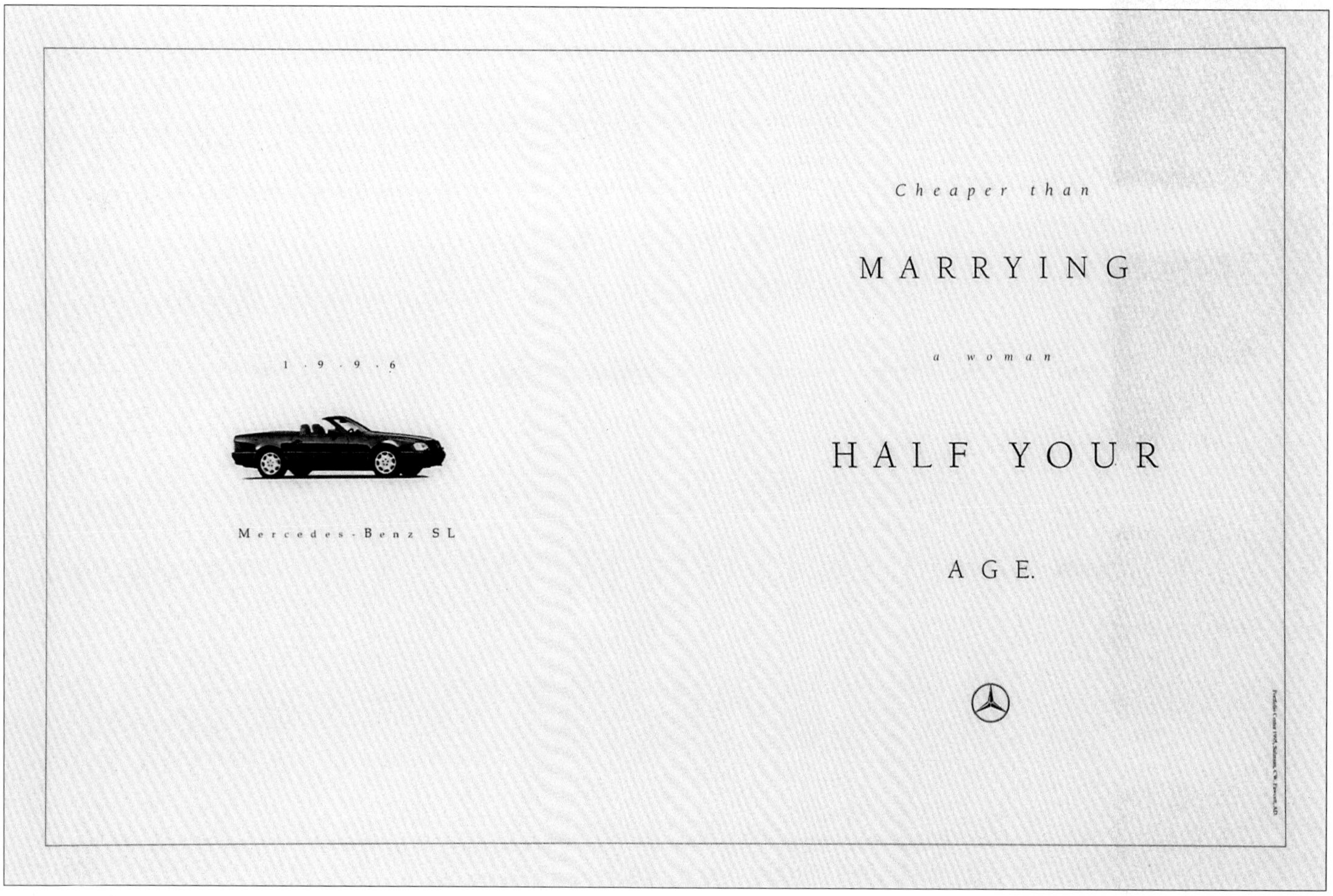

■ *1, 2* **JAY FAWCETT, JARED SALZMAN** *Portfolio Center*

WENN SIE SCHON KEINEN VOLLTREFFER LANDEN KÖNNEN, GÖNNEN SIE SICH WENIGSTENS EINEN APFELSAFT ERSTER WAHL.

CIRO *Die reine Frucht.*

UM KIWIS ZU SEHEN, MÜSSEN SIE SCHON EIN PAAR MARK HINLEGEN. UM KIWI ZU TRINKEN, BRAUCHEN SIE NOCH NICHT MAL EIN GLAS.

CIRO *Die reine Frucht.*

WENN SIE SCHON NICHT WISSEN, WAS DER TAG IHNEN BRINGEN WIRD, MACHEN SIE WENIGSTENS BEIM FRÜHSTÜCK EINE AUSNAHME.

CIRO *Die reine Frucht.*

6

7

8

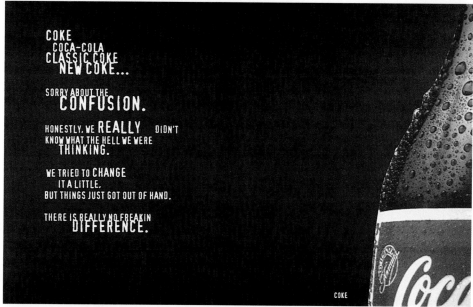

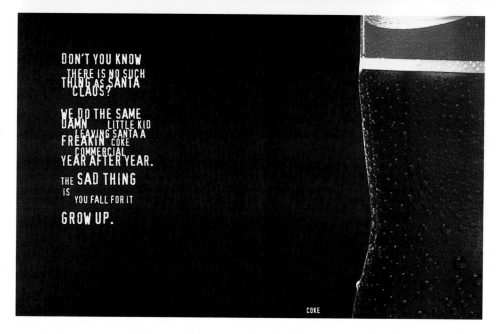

■ *6-8* **KERI ROY** *School of Visual Arts*

Of course you **can** buy
our **beer** from stores,
we **just** don't
think you should
buy a six pack.

IT'S BEEN 141 YRS AND WE'VE ONLY SOLD TWO BEERS.

LIGHT

DARK

WHEN WHAT YOU HAVE IS PERFECT WHY MESS WITH IT?

We suggest **you**
drink your
McSorley's slow,
cause **we** don't
make that much
of it.

8:12 pm

1:58 am

12, 13 **ALEX RODRIGUES** *School of Visual Arts*

14   15

16

■ *14-16* **CHERYL BERNETT, BRAD EISENSTEIN** *University of Delaware*

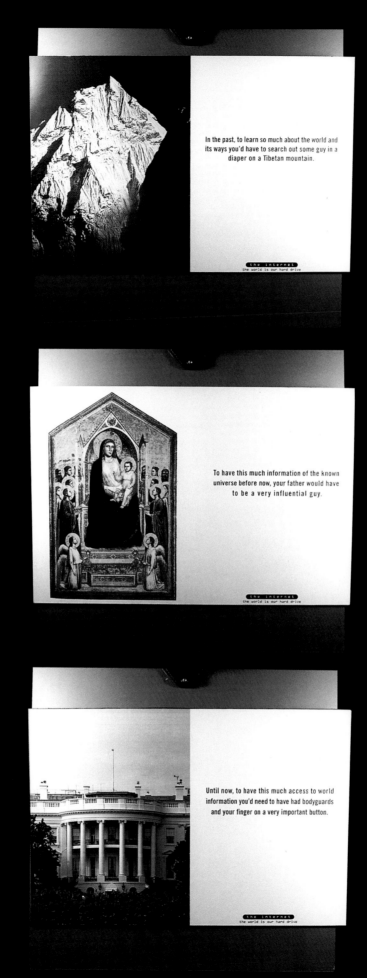

In the past, to learn so much about the world and its ways you'd have to search out some guy in a diaper on a Tibetan mountain.

the internet
the world is our hard drive

To have this much information of the known universe before now, your father would have to be a very influential guy.

the internet
the world is our hard drive

Until now, to have this much access to world information you'd need to have had bodyguards and your finger on a very important button.

the internet
the world is our hard drive

17
18
19

■ *17-19* **MARK TOWNSLEY** *School of Visual Arts*

■ *20-23* **DAVE WASSERMAN** *University of Delaware*

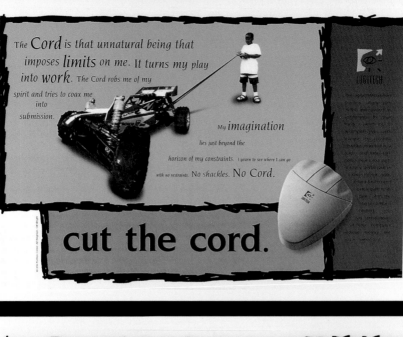
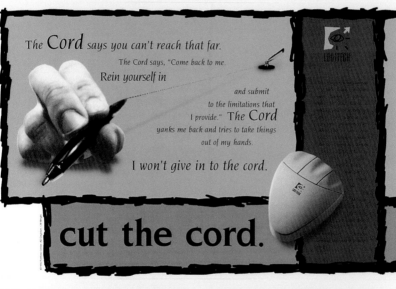
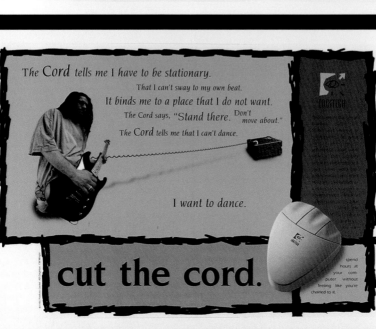

■ *27-29* **CHRIS SAILING, KAREN SCHWARTZ** *Portfolio Center*

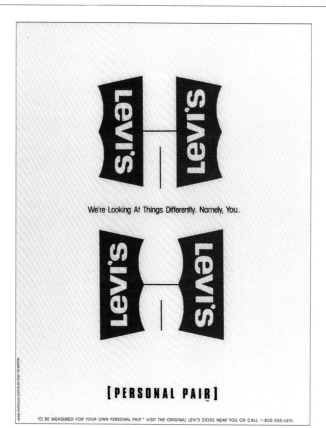

human jeans

it's in your blood.   it's in our jeans.

We're Looking At Things Differently. Namely, You.

[PERSONAL PAIR]

TO BE MEASURED FOR YOUR OWN PERSONAL PAIR™ VISIT THE ORIGINAL LEVI'S STORE NEAR YOU OR CALL 1-800-555-LEVI.

■ *30* **SHAWN BROWN** *Portfolio Center* ■ *31* **SHARON EASTER, NORRIS POST** *Portfolio Center*

30

31

It's unreasonable to think that people who wear Docs aren't clean cut.

Short hair, long hair, no hair. Docs appeal to all types. Maybe it's the durable leather. Or the comfortable AirWair soles. But chances are, it's just the way they look. Because they're not just shoes, they're Docs.

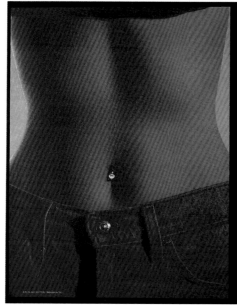

It's unfair to suggest that people who wear Docs don't wear pearls.

What makes Docs a classic accessory? It could be the finely cured leather. Or the comfortable AirWair soles. Odds are, it's just the way they look. Because they're not just shoes, they're Docs.

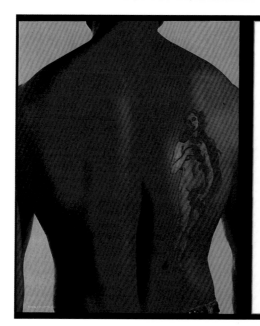

It's wrong to assume that people who wear Docs don't enjoy fine art.

Even the most civilized have an appreciation for Docs. Perhaps it's the hand crafted leather. Or the comfortable AirWair soles. Most likely, it's just the way they look. Because they're not just shoes, they're Docs.

■ *32-34* **SHARON TAO** *Portfolio Center*

We'll open it up and take out its insides!

Anything for your convenience!

We'll bite their ends off!

Anything for your convenience!

We'll poke its eyes out and get under its skin!

Anything for your convenience!

NATURE INTENDS THAT THE RATE OF REPRODUCTION IN A SPECIES IS CONSTANT TO IT'S LIVING CONDITIONS. (DARWIN WROTE THIS REALLY LONG BOOK ON THIS SUBJECT, WHICH IN TURN CAUSED THE DEATH OF RELIGION IN SOME PEOPLE'S MIND, WHATEVER.) ANYWAY, IF YOU REALLY THINK ABOUT IT, SEX WAS NOT INTENDED TO BE FUN. TAKE THE BUNNY RABBIT - THEY CAN REALLY GO AT IT. THEY BREED LIKE THERE'S NO TOMORROW. SOMEHOW THEY FIT INTO THIS EVOLUTIONARY CHAIN, THEY EAT AND GET EATEN. I CAN'T REALLY TELL YOU WHAT THEY EAT, (EXCEPT FOR CARROTS AND MAYBE SOME CHOCOLATE AT EASTER). BUT WHAT I CAN TELL YOU IS THAT I SEE A FEW LAYING ON THE SIDE ON THE ROAD.

SO HOW CAN STARBUCKS BE SEEN ON EVERY STREET CORNER OF THIS FREAKIN' CITY?

LISTEN, NATURE ALLOWS FOR THERE TO BE A BRIEF TIME IN A PERSONS LIFE WHERE HE OR SHE, (YEAH THAT MEANS YOU), SELECTS A MATE SO ONE CAN LIVE LONG AND PROSPER, (AS SPOCK WOULD SAY). JUST FACE IT, WE HUMANS NEED A ROUTINE, NO MATTER HOW STUPID, (LIKE WATCHING MONDAY NIGHT FOOTBALL) TO SURVIVE. ANY ABRUPT CHANGE IN THE HUMAN LIFE CAN REALLY SCREW UP A PERSON IN A BAD WAY. THIS IS WHY WE NEED TO KEEP TO OUR DAILY RITUALS AS CLOSELY AS POSSIBLE.

SO HOW COME, WHEN YOU WALK INTO A STARBUCKS THEY GIVE YOU TOO LARGE, OF A SELECTION TO CHOOSE FROM?

40 41

42 43

44 45

46 47

48 49

■ *46* **BRADFORD EMMETT** *School of Visual Arts* ■ *47-49* **TRACY BULL, MERCY BURWELL, LOIS EILER** *Portfolio Center*

MR. KEITH RICHARDS, HERE IS YOUR RECEIPT.

TOWER RECORDS|VIDEO

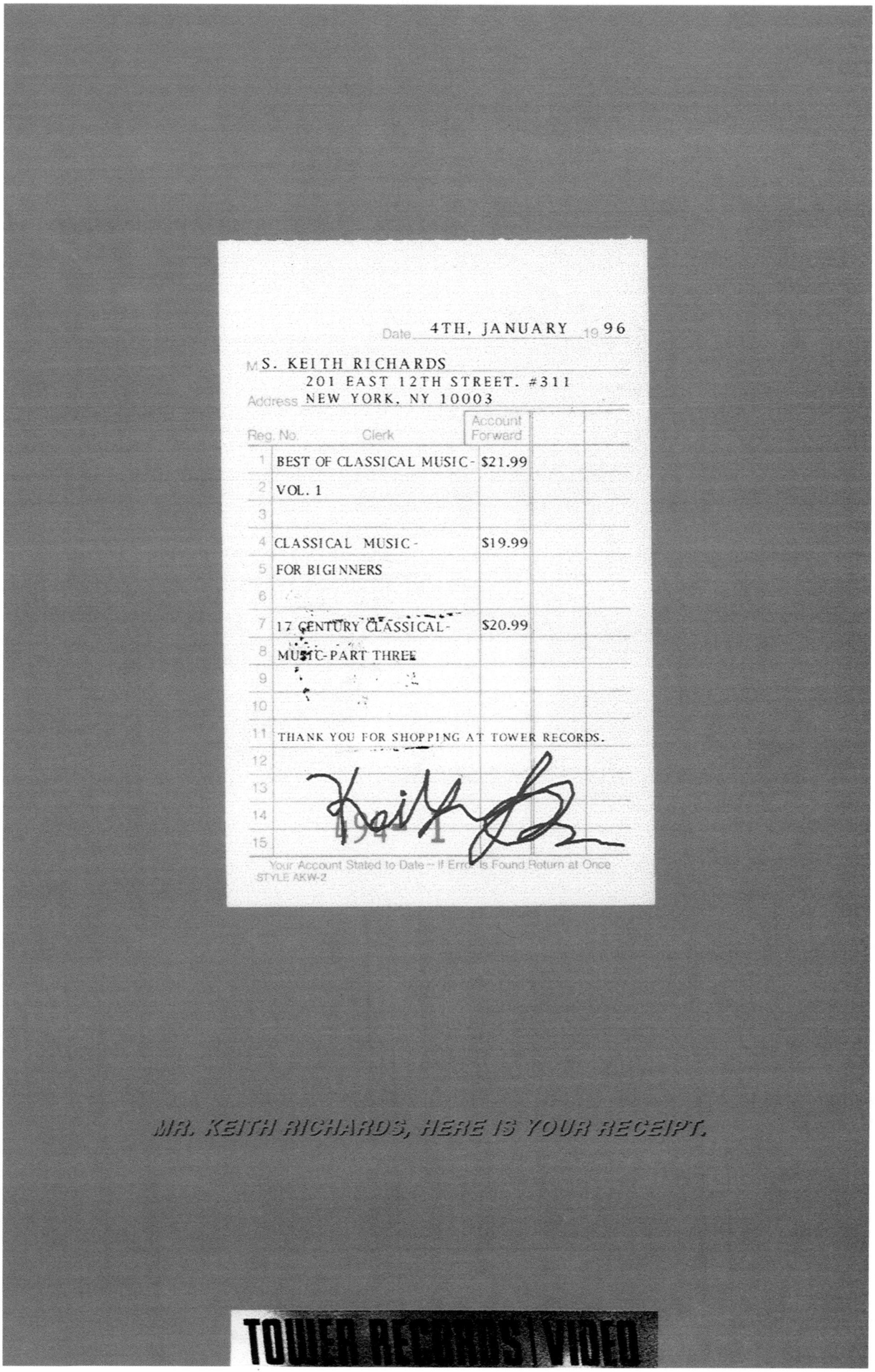

■ *50* **AKI INOUE** *School of Visual Arts*

Songs everyone knows, songs your friends know, and songs no one knows.

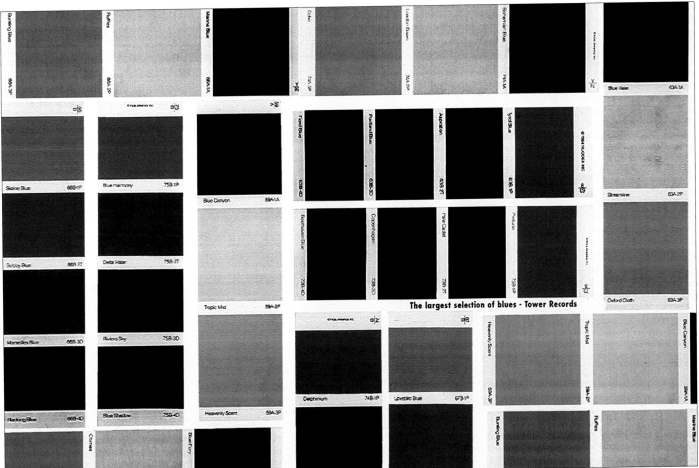

■ *51* **CHRISTOPHER H. YATES** *School of Visual Arts* ■ *52* **KERI ROY** *School of Visual Arts*

53

54

55

■ *53-55* **LENNY MONFREDO** *School of Visual Arts*

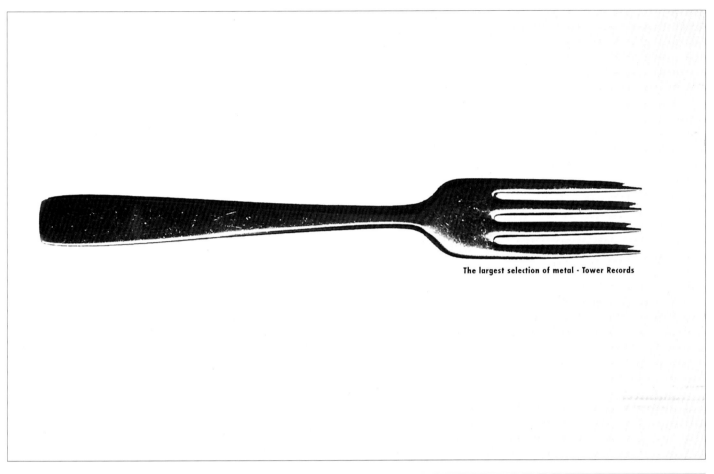

The largest selection of metal - Tower Records

The largest selection of rap - Tower Records

■ *56, 57* **KERI ROY** *School of Visual Arts*

■ *58-61* **KAREN SCHWARTZ, JENNI KELLY** *Portfolio Center*

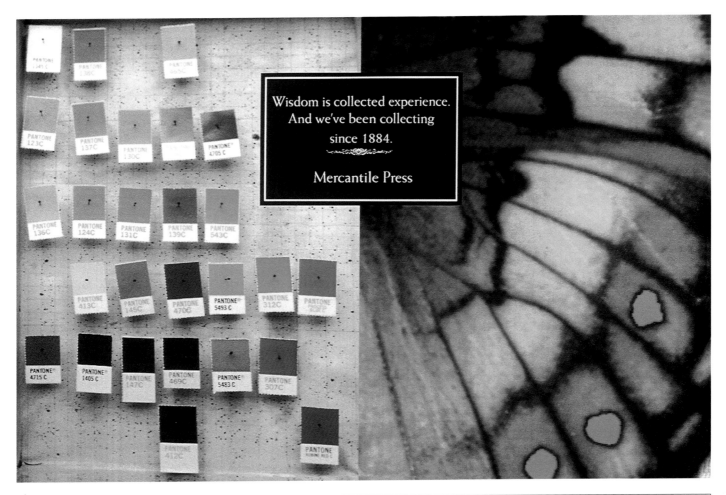

Wisdom is collected experience.
And we've been collecting
since 1884.

Mercantile Press

62

63

PRECISE.
MERCANTILE PRESS

■ *62, 63* **KAREN GERGELY** *University of Delaware*

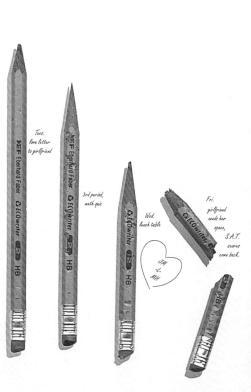

Mon.
S.A.T.'s

Tues.
love letter
to girlfriend

3rd period,
math quiz

Wed.
lunch table

Fri.
girlfriend
needs her
space,
S.A.T.
scores
come back.

The world's number one, number two pencil.

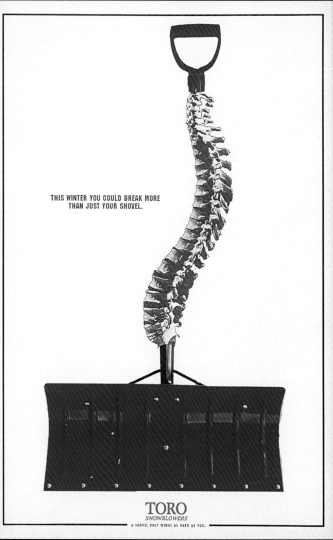

THIS WINTER YOU COULD BREAK MORE
THAN JUST YOUR SHOVEL.

TORO
SNOWBLOWERS

A SHOVEL ONLY WORKS AS HARD AS YOU.

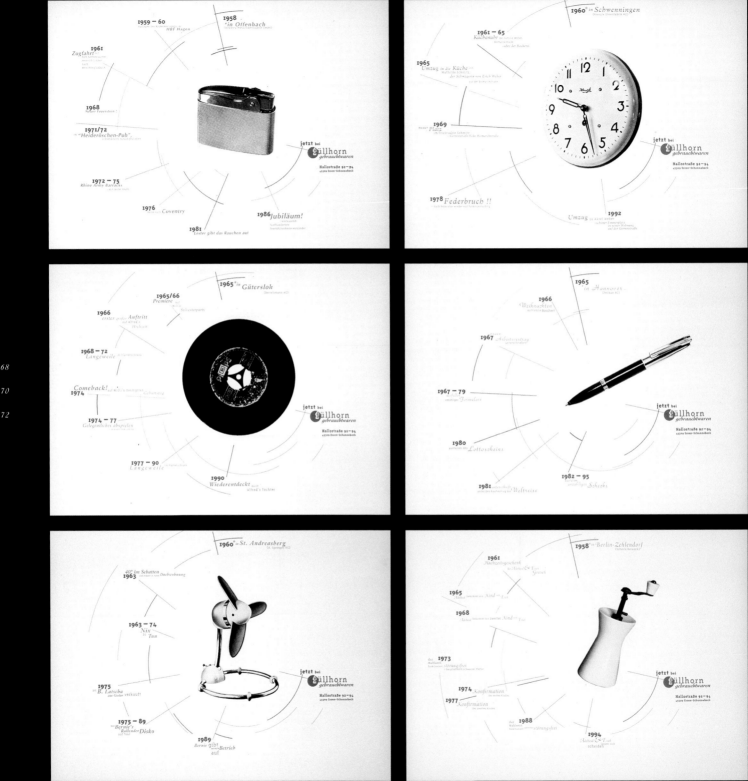

SWISS ARMY

73

74

You fish. Fishing is life, love and liberty. Unfortunately, you can't fish year round. We feel your pain. That's why **Bass Pro Shops Sportsman's Warehouse** has everything you need to satisfy the insatiable urge to dunk a hook into water. Take, for example, our 140,000 gallon fishtank, filled with trophy gamefish. Or our Pro Seminar Series, where you can meet and learn from the gurus. Daily lure demonstrations, tackle out the wazoo, need we say more? Look, we know fishing is a constant state of mind. So think the fish. Feel the fish. Be the fish. Then call **1-800-BASS-PRO** for a location closest to your pond.

Bass Pro Shops

SPORTSMAN'S WAREHOUSE
There is no off-season.

■ *73* **CHRISTIAN BAFFA** *School of Visual Arts* ■ *74* **THOMAS HURD, BRAD KAYE, MICHAEL ZULAWINSKI** *Portfolio Center*

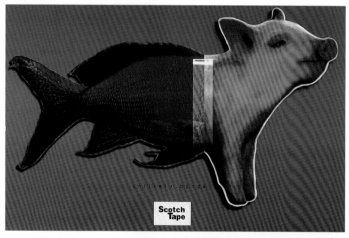

■ 75, 76 **TIM SCHULTHEIS** *School of Visual Arts* ■ 77 **HEATHER PLANSKER** *School of Visual Arts* ■ 78 **TIM SCHULTHEIS** *School of Visual Arts* ■ 79 **FRANK MARTINO** *School of Visual Arts* ■ 80 **LENNY MONFREDO** *School of Visual Arts* ■ 81 **TODD BRUNNER** *School of Visual Arts* ■ 82 **LENNY MONFREDO** *School of Visual Arts*

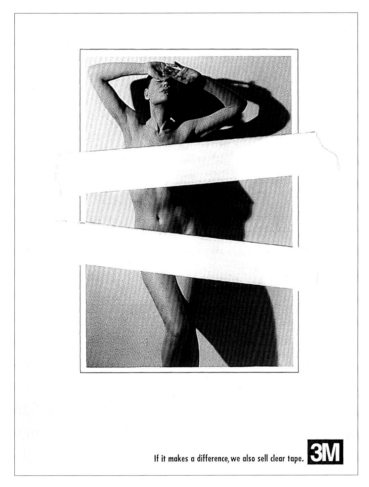

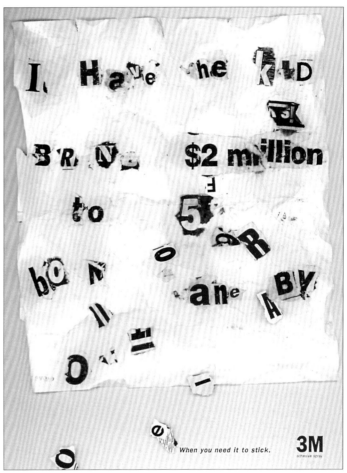

83   84

■ *83* **MARCO MORSELLA** *School of Visual Arts* ■ *84* **LAUREN S. BARROCAS** *School of Visual Arts*

85

86

■ *85* **BRADFORD EMMETT** *School of Visual Arts* ■ *86* **LENNY MONFREDO** *School of Visual Arts*

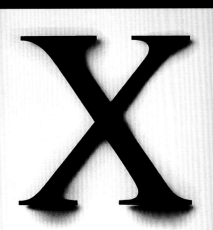

Ein Ypsilon.

Lesen, denken,
mitgestalten.
Eine Aktion der
Zeitungen in Deutschland.

Ein Nagel.

Lesen, denken,
mitgestalten.
Eine Aktion der
Zeitungen in Deutschland.

Eine Birne.

Lesen, denken,
mitgestalten.
Eine Aktion der
Zeitungen in Deutschland.

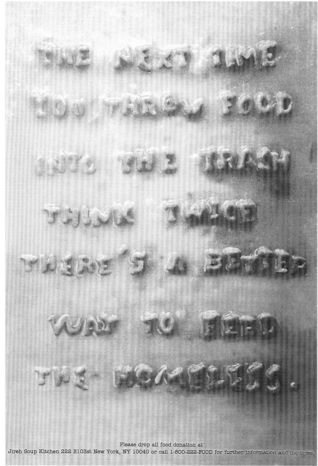

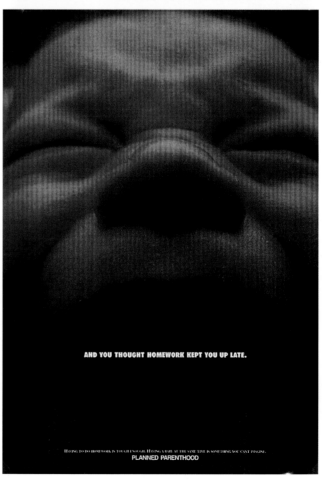

90 91

92 93

■ *90* **DANA BETGILAN** *School of Visual Arts* ■ *91* **MEI YAP** *School of Visual Arts* ■ *92, 93* **KERI ROY** *School of Visual Arts*

94

**CHILDREN'S ALCOHOL ABUSE HOTLINE
1-800-252-6465**

■ *94* **CRAIG GHIGLIONE** *Portfolio Center*

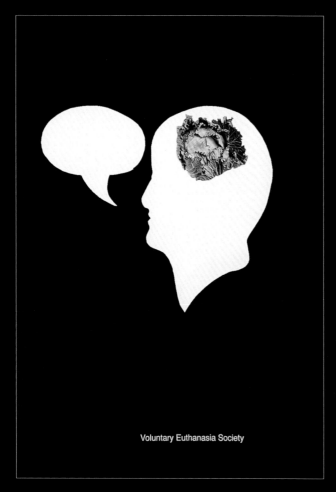

Voluntary Euthanasia Society

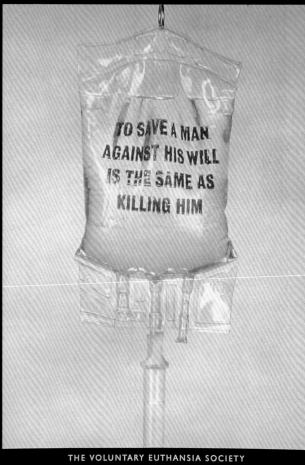

THE VOLUNTARY EUTHANSIA SOCIETY

■ *95* **SARAH CLACKSON** *Somerset College of Arts and Technology* ■ *96* **JAMES FOSS** *Somerset College of Arts and Technology*
■ *97, 98* **REBECCA EDWARDS** *Somerset College of Arts and Technology*

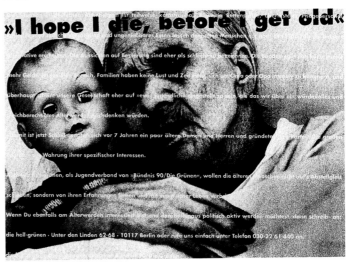

■ *99-104* **JAN KOEMMET** *Bergische Universität Wuppertal*

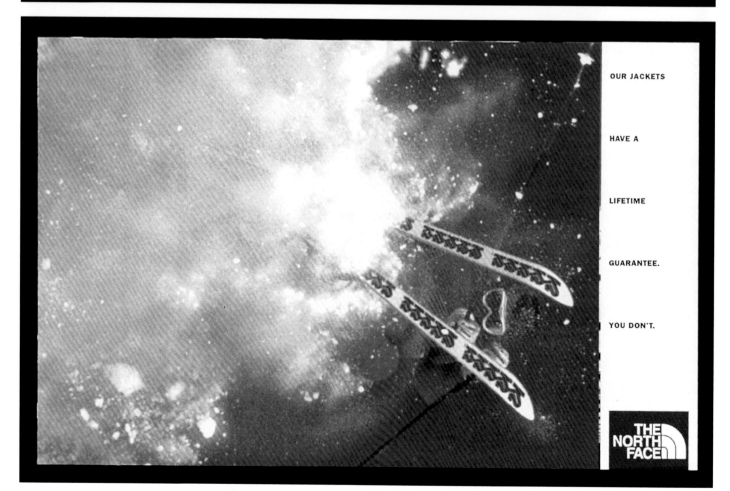

105

106

■ *105, 106* **LAUREN S. BARROCAS** *School of Visual Arts*

107

108

■ *107* **MARK TOWNSLEY** *School of Visual Arts* ■ *108* **TIM SCHULTHEIS** *School of Visual Arts*

you need some **clothes?**

Second-Skin ©
thermal suit

SUPERMODEL SNOWBOARDS PRESENTS

③ new**super**models

Fs.0001 **kate**

model Hb.0002 **cindy**

for**winter**⁹⁷

model Team.0003 **christy**

2307 WILSHIRE BLVD LOS ANGELES CA90057 TEL(213)389.6008 FAX(213)389.7000

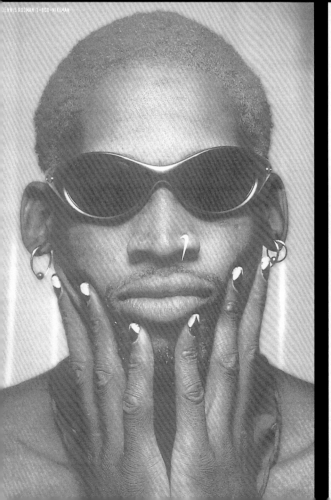

DENNIS RODMAN 1-800-NIKEMAN

WALKMAN( )
MAILMAN( )
RODMAN(✓)

DENNIS RODMAN
1-800-NIKEMAN

■ *113* **BRADFORD EMMETT** *School of Visual Arts*

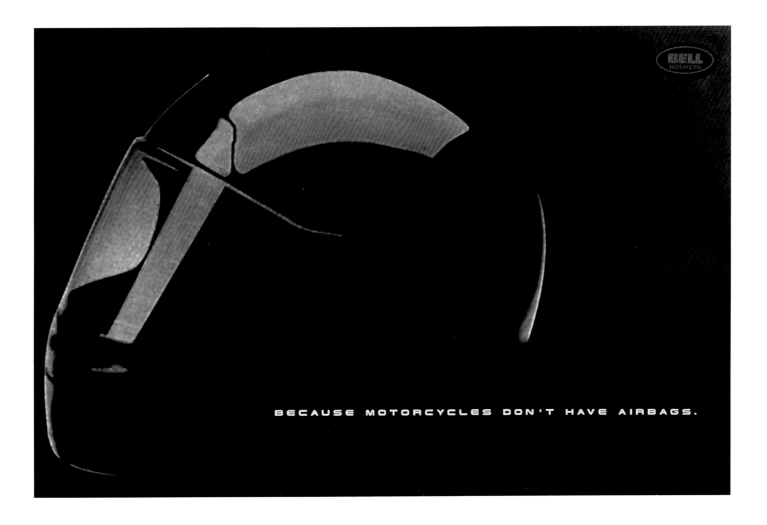

113

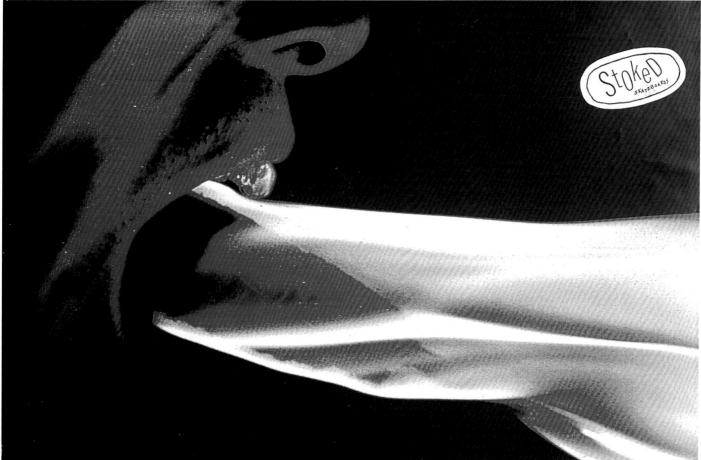

■ *117* **KEVIN STOOHS** *School of Visual Arts* ■ *118* **TIM SCHULTHEIS** *School of Visual Arts*

(THIS SPREAD) ■ *119-130* **LUTZ WIDMAIER** *Staatliche Akademie der Bildenden Künste*

131 132

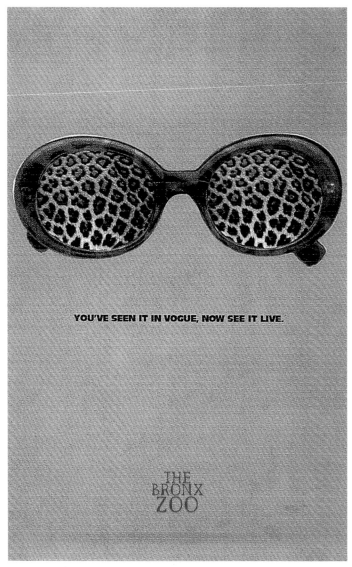

COME DO SOME LINES WITH US.

YOU'VE SEEN IT IN VOGUE, NOW SEE IT LIVE.

■ *131, 132* **SIBILA DEL MAR MUNOZ** *School of Visual Arts*

133

134

■ *133, 134* **TOM DOWD** *School of Visual Arts*

■ *135* **AKI INOUE** *School of Visual Arts*

Der erste Indianer war ein Sauerländer.

Germany

Von der Ostsee ging's direkt nach Troja.

Germany

In Thüringen macht man Ihnen schöne Augen.

Germany

007 beichtet inkognito in Hessen.

Germany

Ayers Rock in Schleswig-Holstein.

Germany

Im Schwarzwald gingen die Römer baden.

Germany

Sachsen-Anhalt ist der Mittelpunkt der Erde.

Germany

Die Apollo-14-Expedition startete auf der Schwäbischen Alb.

Germany

■ *136-143* **THIMOTEUS IBYKUS WAGNER** *Universität FH Essen*

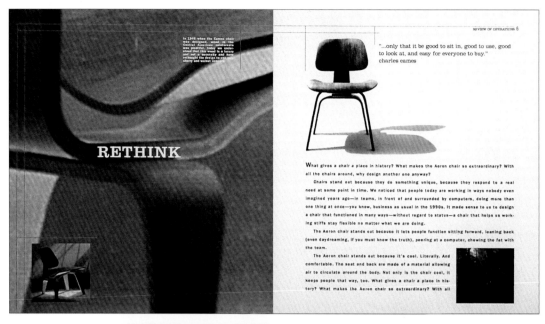

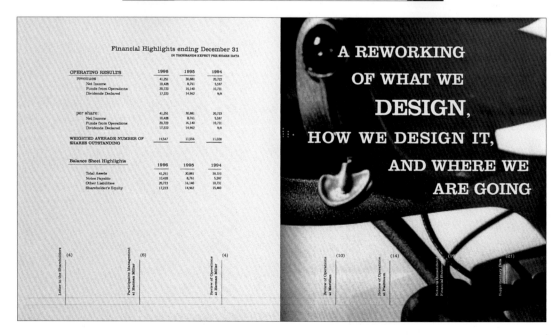

144

145

146

■ *144-146* **JEFF DEY** *University of North Texas*

BUSINESS REPLY MAIL
FIRST CLASS PERMIT NO. 2207 NEW YORK, NEW YORK

POSTAGE WILL BE PAID BY ADDRESSEE

GRAPHIS U.S. INC.

141 LEXINGTON AVENUE

NEW YORK, NEW YORK 10157-0236

FREE CATALOGUE
....

YOUR OPINION WOULD BE HELPFUL TO US. PLEASE COMPLETE THIS CARD AND RECEIVE A FREE GRAPHIS CATALOGUE.

BOOK TITLE _____ AUTHOR _____

WHAT DID YOU LIKE (OR NOT LIKE)? _____

_____

_____

WHAT DID YOU FIND MOST USEFUL? _____

_____

PURCHASED AT: _____ YOUR PROFESSION: _____

I AM INTERESTED IN: ☐ GRAPHIC DESIGN ☐ PHOTOGRAPHY ☐ ILLUSTRATION ☐ ADVERTISING ☐ TYPOGRAPHY

☐ PACKAGE DESIGN ☐ ARCHITECTURE/INTERIOR DESIGN ☐ POSTER ☐ PRODUCT DESIGN

NAME _____ COMPANY _____

ADDRESS _____

CITY _____ STATE _____ ZIP _____

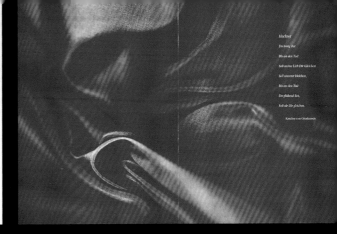

Hochrot

Du treug Rot
Bis an den Tod
Soll meine Lieb Dir gleichen
Soll nimmer bleichen,
Bis an den Tod
Du glühend Rot,
Soll sie Dir gleichen.

Kanzlino von Glockenton

Ode an die Rose

An die Rote
an diese Rose
die einzige
an den schwebende erscheinene
rote Rose
an den sanfteste Tiefe
in das Äußersten ihres Schoßes
rot.

Pablo Neruda

Rot als Farbe der Fruchtbarkeit.

»Rote Haare, Sommersprossen, sind des Teufels Artgenossen«

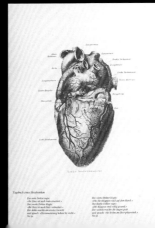

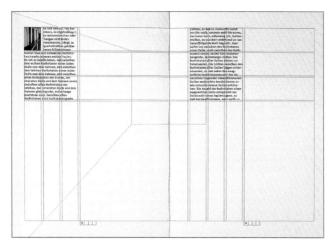

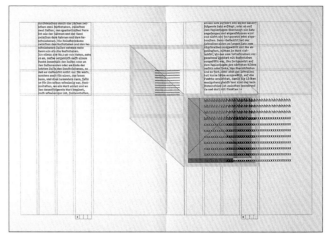

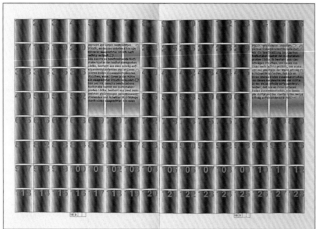

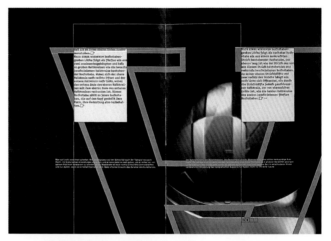

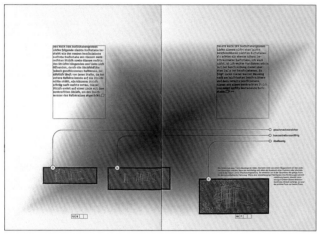

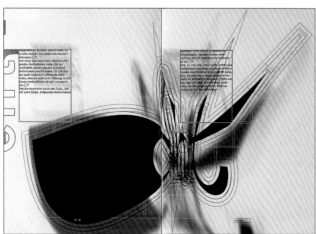

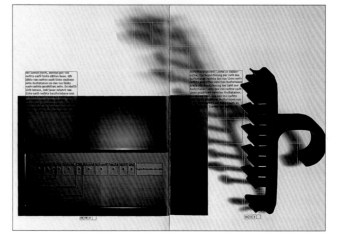

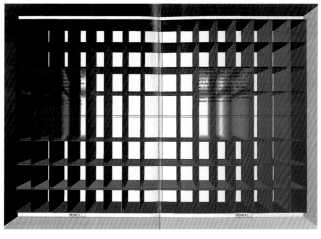

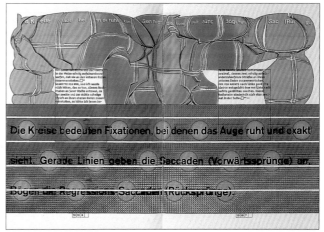

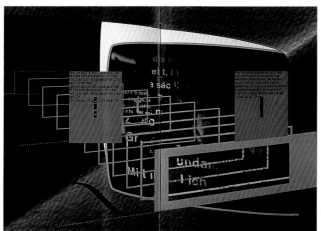

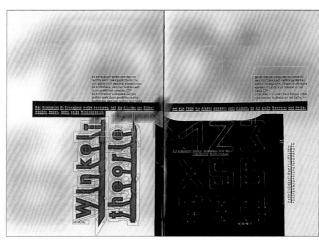

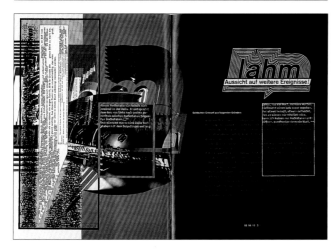

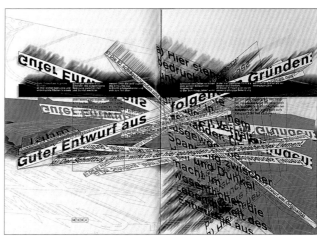

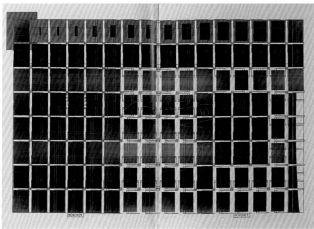

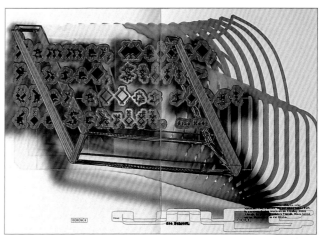

(THIS SPREAD) ■ 155-170 **GROUP PROJECT** *Staatliche Akademie der Bildenden Künste*

S T A R N

MIKE AND DOUG

174

175

176

■ *174* **SHA-MAYNE CHAN** *School of Visual Arts* ■ *175* **GROUP PROJECT** *Staatliche Akademie der Bildenden Künste* ■ *176* **SO TAKAHASHI** *School of Visual Arts*

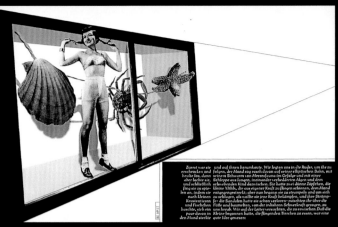

Fast ähnelte er dem Bauch eines Fisches, und wenn ich mich recht erinnere, roch er auch so

naja, vielleicht nicht gerade direkt wie ein Fisch, aber kaum weniger streng, etwa so wie geräucherter Lachs. In Wirklichkeit konnte man ihn nur von der Leiter aus, wenn man sich balancierend auf die oberste Sprosse stellte und die Arme ausstreckte, gerade erreichen. Wir hatten gut Maß genommen (wir ahnten ja noch nicht, daß er sich langsam entfernte). Das einzige, was man genau bedenken mußte, war die Stelle, wo man ihn anfaßte.

Zuerst war sie und auf ihnen herumkaute. Wir legten uns in die Ruder, um sie zu erschrecken: erst fielen, der Mond zog nach davon auf seiner elliptischen Bahn, mit heulte los, dann seinem Schwarm von Meeresfauna im Gefolge und mit einer aber hörte sie, Schleppe aus langen, ineinander verschederten Algen und dem und schließlich schwebenden Kind dazwischen. Sie hatte nur dünne Zapfchen, die fing sie zu spie-kleine Xhhs, die aus eigener Kraft zu fliegen schienen, dem Mond...

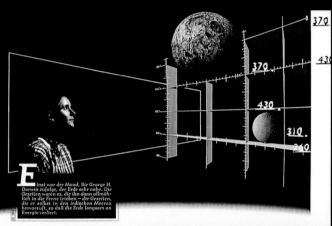

Einst war der Mond, Sir George H. Darwin zufolge, der Erde sehr nahe. Die Gezeiten waren es, die ihn daran allmählich in die Ferne trieben — die Gezeiten, die er selbst in den irdischen Meeren hervorruft, so daß die Erde langsam an Energie verliert.

Auf dem Mond gab es weite Regionen, die zu erkunden uns nie ein Anlaß oder eine Neugier gegeben hatte; dort pflegte mein Vetter dann zu verschwinden...

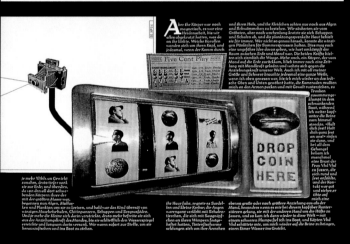

Aber ihr Körper war noch magnetisch, es war eine Heidenarbeit, wir die alles abgekratzt hatten, was da an ihr klebte. Weiche Korallen wanden sich um ihren Kopf, und jedesmal, wenn der Raum durch begannen aus Algen, Mollus...

Je mehr Xhhs an Gewicht zunahm, desto tiefer sank sie zur Erde und überdies, da sein den alt zwei schwebenden Körpern ihrer der mit der größten Masse war, begannen aus Algen, Mollus...

Five Cent Play

DROP COIN HERE

Ständig schwirrte allerlei Kleingetier durch die Luft: winzige Krebse und Tintenfische, ...

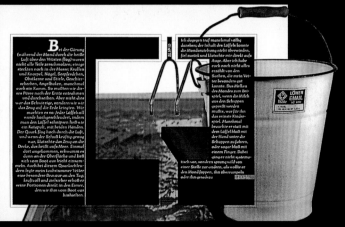

Bei der Gärung (während der Mond durch die heiße Luft über den Wüsten flog) waren nicht alle Teile geschmolzen, einige steckten noch in der Masse: Krallen und Knorpel, Nägel, Seepferdchen, Obstkerne und Stiele, Angelhaken, Angelhaken, manchmal auch ein Kamm. So mußten wir die...

Ich dagegen traf manchmal völlig daneben; der Inhalt des Löffels konnte die Mondanziehung nicht überwinden, fiel zurück und klatschte mir direkt aufs Auge. Aber ich habe euch noch nicht alles erzählt von den...

Sie fanden sofort die richtige Stelle zum Anfassen, wo es sich anfassen konnte, ja es schien fast, als ob er durch den Boden Druck seiner Handflächen an der Mondkruste haftete...

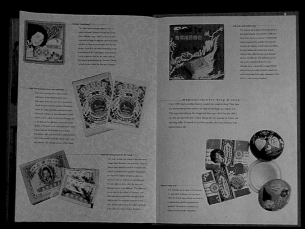

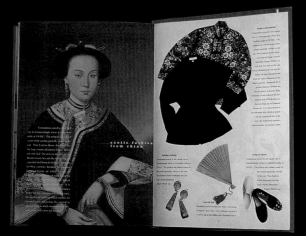

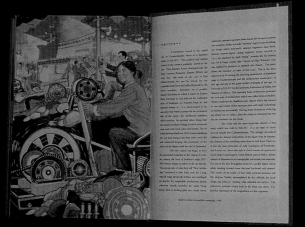

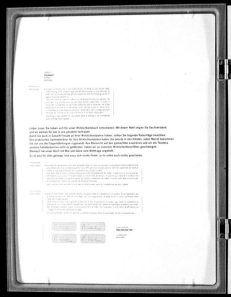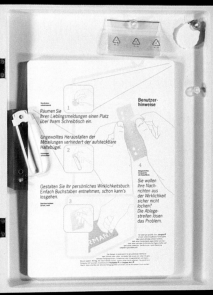

■ *200* **HUBIE LE** *Portfolio Center* ■ *201-202* **MARCUS WICHMANN** *Staatliche Akademie der Bildenden Künste*

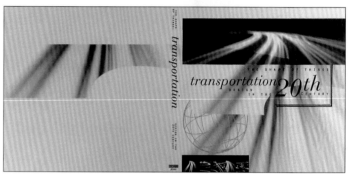

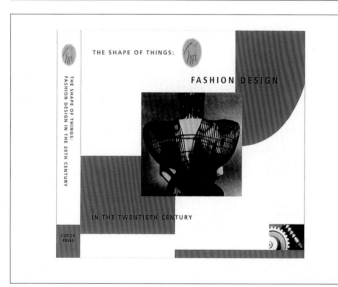

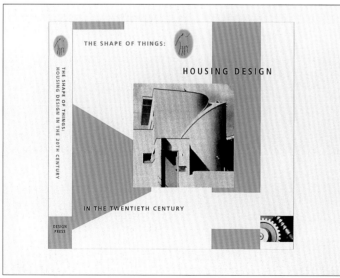

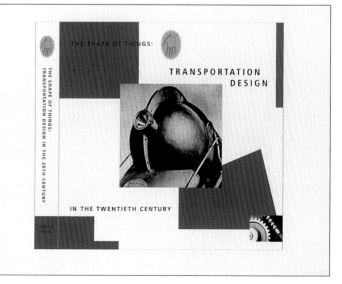

■ *203-206* **ANDREW REED** *Oregon State University* ■ *207-210* **AMIE WALTER** *Oregon State University*

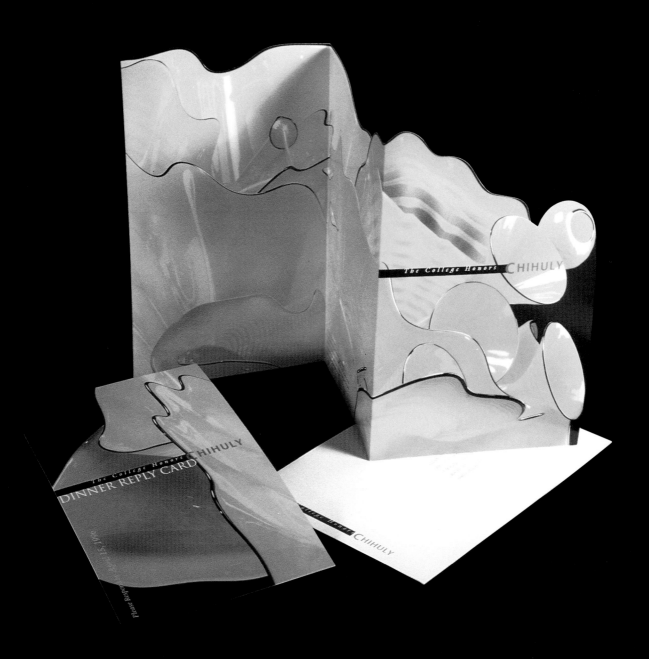

■ *211* **CONNIE M. HWANG** *University of Washington*

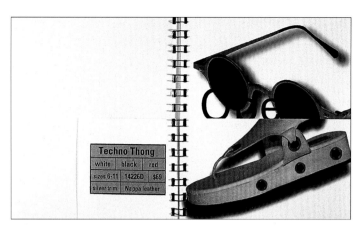

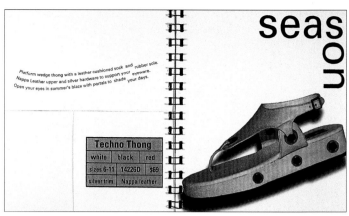

season

Platform wedge thong with a leather cushioned sock and rubber sole.
Nappa Leather upper and silver hardware to support your eyeware.
Open your eyes in summer's blaze with portals to shade your days.

Techno Thong

white	black	red
sizes 6-11	14226D	$69
silver trim	Nappa leather	

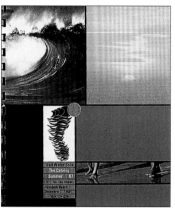

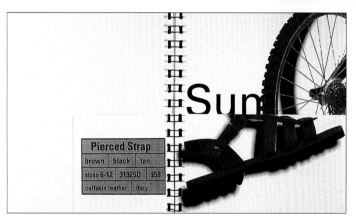

Sum

Pierced Strap

brown	black	tan
sizes 6-12	31925D	$58
calfskin leather	Italy	

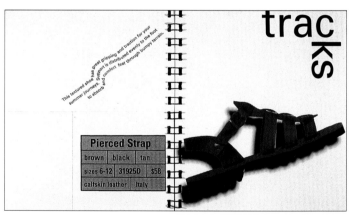

tracks

This textured shoe has great gripping and traction for your
summer journeys. Support is distributed evenly to the foot
to absorb and comfort feet through bumpy terrain.

Pierced Strap

brown	black	tan
sizes 6-12	31925D	$58
calfskin leather	Italy	

Natu**res**

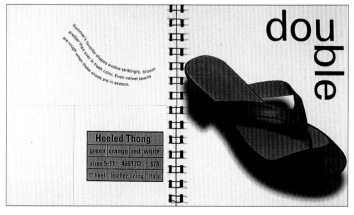

double

Summer's favorite shapes evolve strikingly, bloom
prettier than ever in fresh color. Even velvet lawns
are rough when these shoes are in season.

Heeled Thong

green	orange	red	white
sizes 5-11	46617D	$78	
1" heel	leather lining	Italy	

■ *212-218* **ANDRIA DAVIS, ABIGAIL FEIN** *University of Delaware*

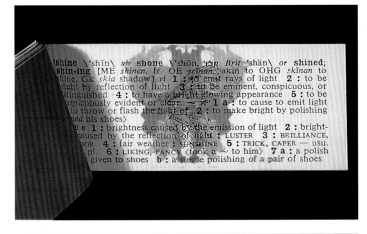 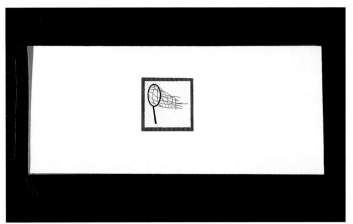

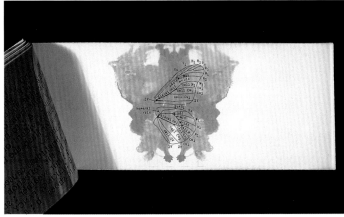 

 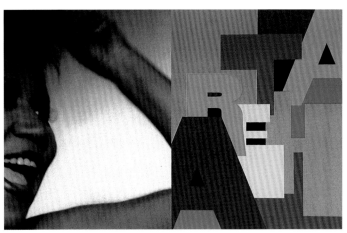

■ *219-222* **ABIGAIL FEIN** *University of Delaware* ■ *223* **GABRIEL KUO** *School of Visual Arts* ■ *224, 225* **INGRID FORBORD** *School of Visual Arts*

■ 226, 227 **GEOFF KAPLAN** *Cranbrook Academy of Art*

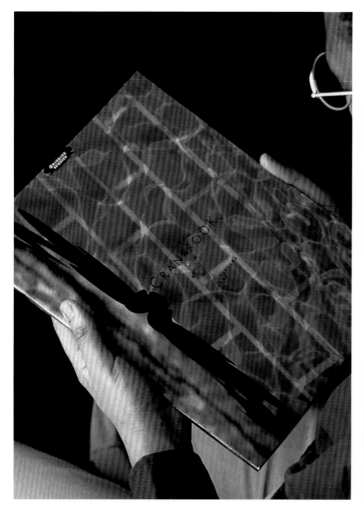

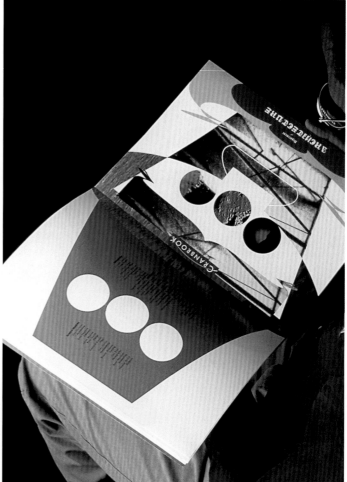

■ *226, 227* **GEOFF KAPLAN** *Cranbrook Academy of Art*

VOLUME

response | 27

the museum of tolerance newsletter

March 1995

*This issue features
an article by
Professor Cornel West
and poems by
Maya Angelou
and Langston Hughes*

a free bird leaps. on the back of the wind.

he can seldom see through his bars of rage his wings are clipped and his feet are tied. so he opens his throat to sing.

but a bird that stalks. down his narrow cage.

and his tune is heard. on the distant hill. for the caged bird. sings of freedom.

MAYA ANGELOU

is the author of the best-selling I KNOW WHY THE CAGED
BIRDS SING, GATHER TOGETHER IN MY NAME, *and* THE HEART
OF A WOMAN, *she has also written five collections of poetry,
and* I SHALL NOT BE MOVED, *as well as* ON THE PULSE OF THE
MORNING, *which was read by her at the inauguration of
President William Jefferson Clinton on January 20, 1993.*

229

■ *229* **TIM ROGERS** *University of South Australia*

230 231

232 233

234 235

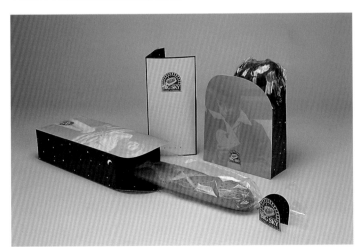

■ *230, 231* **GILMAR WENDT** *Fachhochschule Mainz* ■ *232* **REGINA KRUTOY** *School of Visual Arts* ■ *233* **MICHAEL TOMPERT** *Academy of Art College*
■ *234* **KELLY HOLOHAN** *Tyler School of Art* ■ *235* **ANGELA SCHROEDER** *Fachhochschule Mainz*

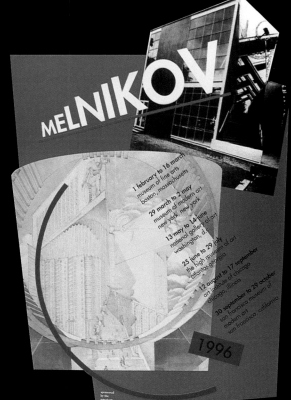

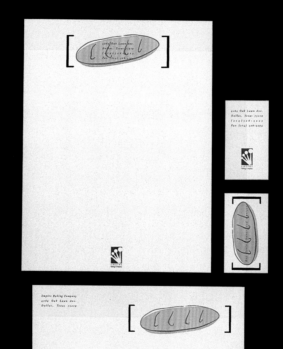

241 242

243

244 245

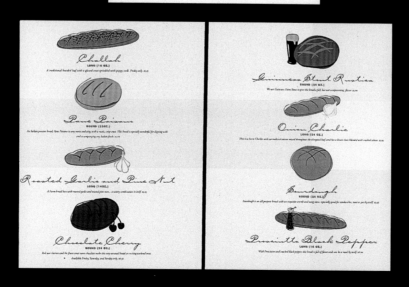

■ *241-245* **AMANDA M. POUNDS** *University of North Texas*

246

■ *246* **TARA BENYEI** *Academy of Art College*

MUSIC ART FASHION

WORLD

JUNE 20 1996 $3.95

LIGHTS UP

MORE SOAP | LA NOVELA CONTINUES

METHOD MAN

Drugs, Prison or Death Drugs, Prison or Death Drugs, Prison or Death Drugs, Prison or Death Drugs, Prison or Death

247

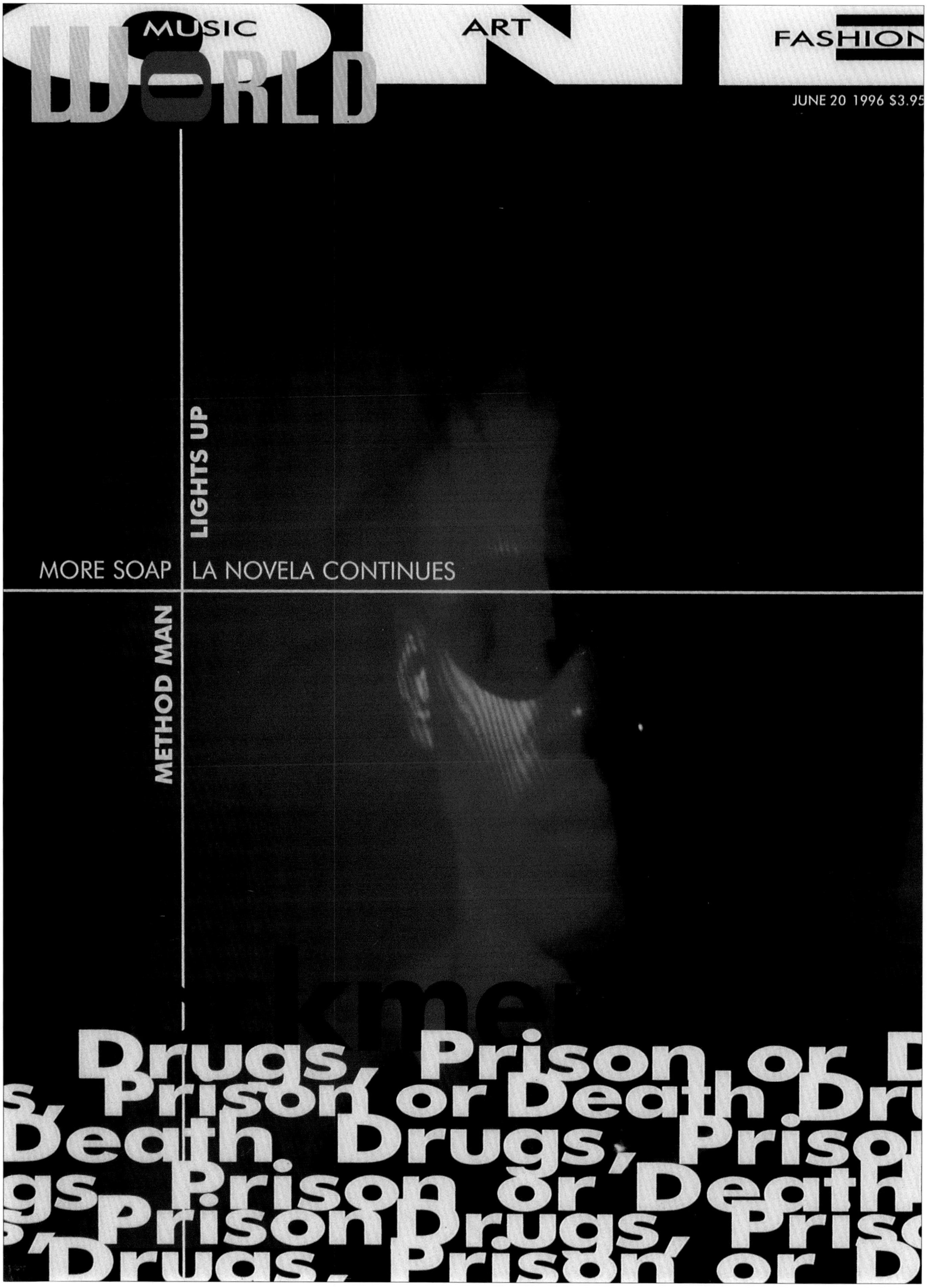

■ *247* **STEVE CLIFTON** *Portfolio Center*

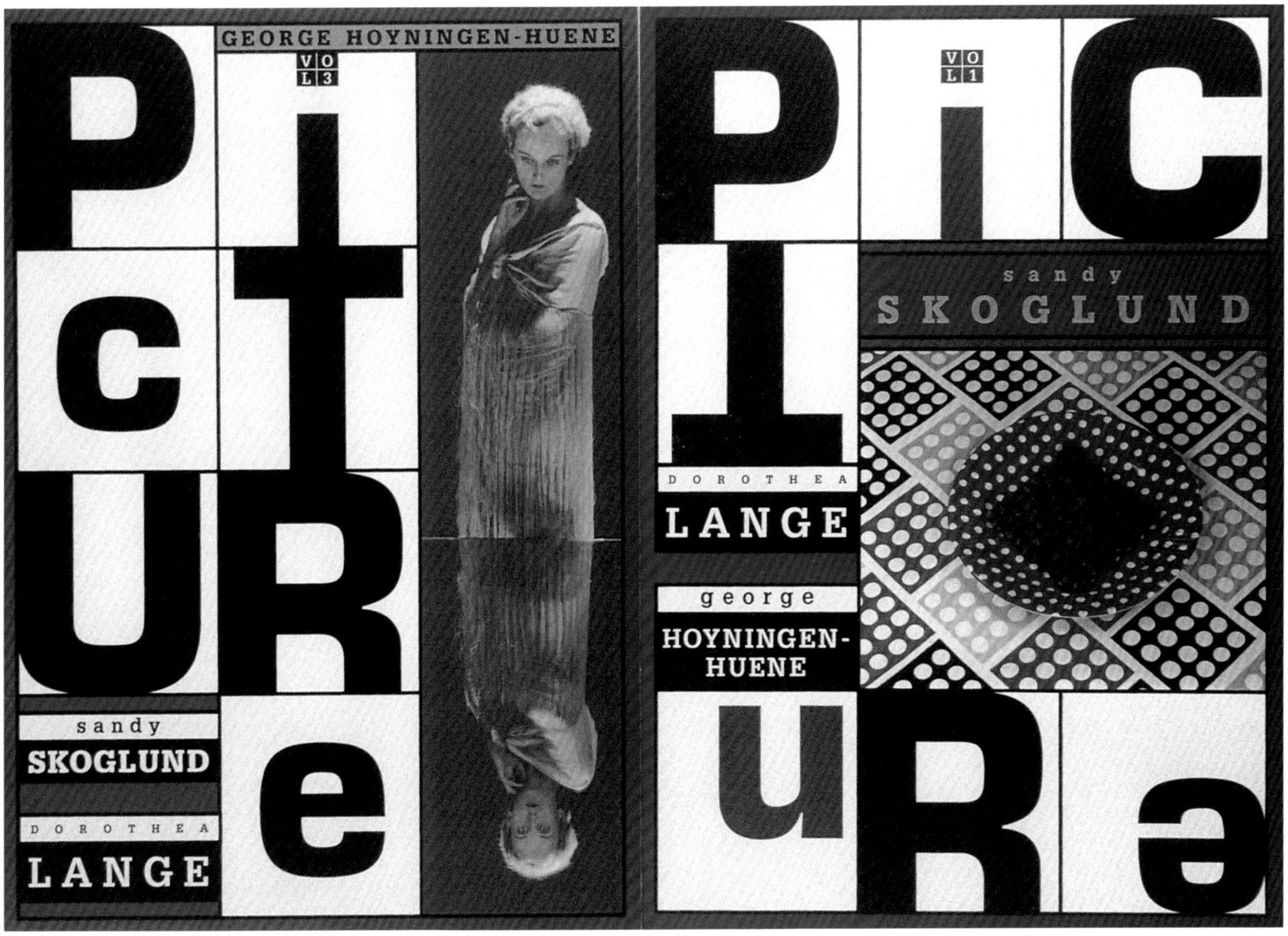

■ *248* **SUZANNE ACH** *School of Visual Arts*

249 250
251 252
253 254

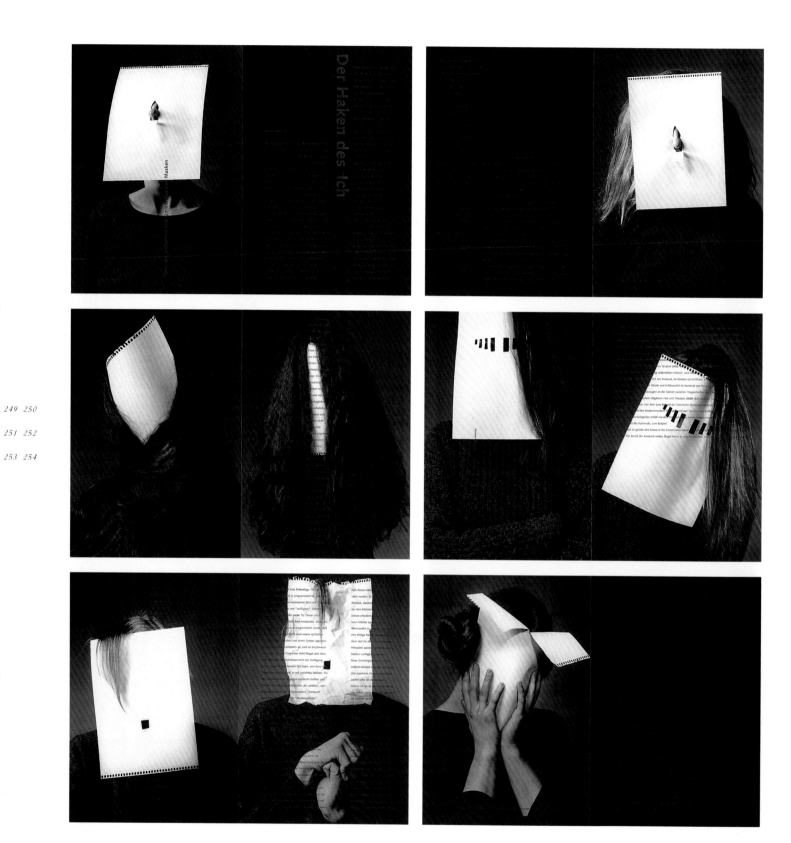

■ *249-254* **KERSTIN HAMBURG** *Bergische Universität Wuppertal*

ABOUT THIS ISSUE...

SEBASTIÃO SALGADO CREATES A MOVING, EXTRAORDINARY HUMAN DOCUMENT OF THE BEAUTY AND STRENGTH OF PEOPLE IN THE DEEPEST, MOST ABOMINABLE KIND OF SUFFERING. MAN RAY EMBRACES, SURREALISM AND DADAISM, CREEDS THAT EMPHASIZES CHANCE EFFECTS, DISJUNCTION AND SURPRISE. GEORGE HOYNINGEN-HUENE MADE AN OUTSTANDING CONTRIBUTION TO FASHION PHOTOGRAPHY. THE KEY TO HUENE'S ACHIEVEMENT LIES IN THE CONSISTENCY, INTELLECTUAL COMPLEXITY, AND INTER-RELATEDENESS OF HIS IDEAS.

LET THE TRUTH BE THE PREJUDICE

PHOTOGRAPHS BY
SEBASTIÃO SALGADO

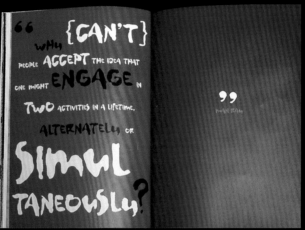

"WHY {CAN'T} PEOPLE ACCEPT THE IDEA THAT ONE MIGHT ENGAGE IN TWO ACTIVITIES IN A LIFETIME, ALTERNATELY OR SIMULTANEOUSLY?"

GEORGE HOYNINGEN-HUENE

263 264

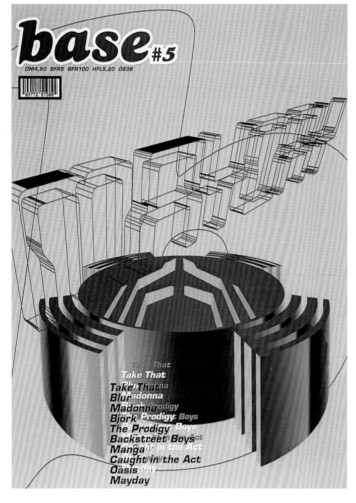

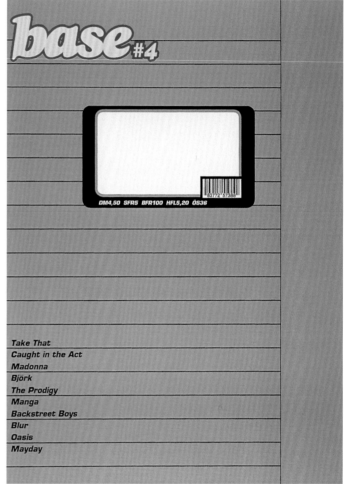

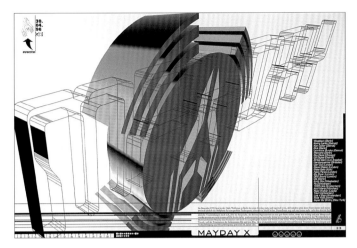

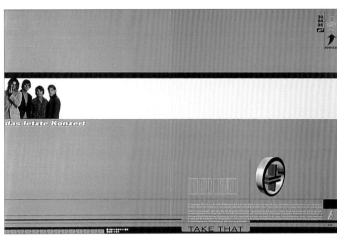

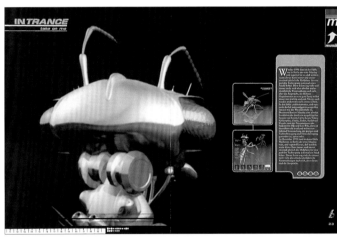

■ *265-271* **INGO DITGES** *Staatliche Akademie der Bildenden Künste* ■ *272* **KARIN KAISER** *Staatliche Akademie der Bildenden Künste*

ZANK Apfel!

Es ist typographischen Laien nämlich oft gar nicht klarzumachen, daß es Sinn und Zweck hat, so viel Arbeit und auch Liebe auf das Zeichnen dieser kleinen Buchstaben zu verwenden, die, kaum überflogen, schon zusammengeknüllt im Papierkorb landen. Wie gesagt, so argumentiert der Laie. Der Fachmann hingegen erkennt die feinsinnigen Unterschiede zwischen den Schriften und weiß wohl um ihre Wirkung auf den Betrachter. Ist es doch mit der Typografie wie mit den anderen Künsten: dem Abomogdowen muß auf die Sprünge geholfen werden und bald eröffnet sich ihm eine neue, abenteuerliche Welt, eine Welt, erfüllt mit Gegenständen für den geistigen Gebrauch. Aber was öffnet dem Abonogdowen die Augen für die blühende Wiese der Typografie? Warum gibt es eigentlich keine Typografiekritiker? Jeden Morgen lese ich in der Zeitung Kritiken über alle möglichen Veranstaltungen des Vorabends: Theater, Film, Musik

Geschichten aus dem Paradies und anderen Gärten.

Auf den Abhängen des Berges Atlas, wo die keuchenden Wagenpferde der Sonne ihre Reise vollenden, liegen die Gärten des Abendsterns, die Gärten der Hera. Obwohl die Äpfel Hera gehörten, hegte Atlas für sie den Stolz eines Gärtners, baute feste Mauern um den Fruchtgarten und vertrieb alle Eindringlinge. Als jedoch Herakles zum Garten kam, bat er Atlas, ihm einen Gefallen zu tun während ihn von seiner Last befreie. Atlas hätte dafür jede Aufgabe auf sich genommen. Herakles tötete die Schlange Ladon, die die Äpfel bewachte, mit einem Pfeilschuß, nahm Atlas die himmlische Wölbung ab und dieser brachte ihm drei der Äpfel, die die drei Hesperiden, die Hüterinnen des Gartens gepflückt hatten. So kam Herakles in den Besitz der goldenen Äpfel.

A T O L L

Es ist angerichtet!

ATOLL 4 97

A T O L L

Frau [sic. femmes eller..., (lateinisch), weibl. erwachsener Mensch. Die Wesensdefinition der F. variiert je nach geograph. Raum, kleine Epoche sowie Gesellschafts- und Kulturtypus. Die zuldemittelbari Anteil an der Rev. ist literaturspezifisch ausschließlich.

ATOLL 2 97

Liebe, Geld und Tod Ritterspiele Liebesspiele Psychospiele die Glücks-fee Verlierer (ewige) Lebens-künstler Zufall Zocker Zirkus ein Schauspie... z & Maus das Kind im M... der Automat

homo ludens der spielende Mensch

ATOLL 5 97

Es ist typographischen Laien nämlich oft gar nicht klarzumachen, daß es Sinn und Zweck hat, so viel Arbeit und auch Liebe auf das Zeichnen dieser kleinen Buchstaben zu verwenden, die, kaum überflogen, schon zusammengeknüllt im Papierkorb landen. Wie gesagt, so argumentiert der Laie. Der Fachmann **Auszeichnung für ihren Helden.** Die Unterschiede zwischen den Schriften und weiß wohl um ihre Wirkung auf den Betrachter. Ist es doch mit der Typografie wie mit den anderen Künsten: dem Abomogdowen muß auf die Sprünge geholfen werden und bald eröffnet sich ihm eine neue, abenteuerliche Welt, eine Welt, erfüllt mit Gegenständen für den geistigen Gebrauch. Aber was öffnet dem Abonogdowen die Augen für die blühende Wiese der Typografie? Warum gibt es eigentlich keine Typografiekritiker? Jeden Morgen lese ich in der Zeitung Kritiken über alle möglichen Veranstaltungen des Vorabends: Theater, Film, Musik, Ja, sogar das Fernsehen werden einer kritischen Würdigung verrissen. Ja, von hauptberuflichen Architekturkritikern lese man gelegentlich, wie wenig Einfluß der Kritiker auf den Gang der kulturellen Dinge im allgemeinen hat. Und ein weiteres, verweifeltes Manko dieses Berufsstandes offenbart offenbart sich aus augenfälliger

„Der Liebesgöttin einen Apfel zu überreichen, wäre eine Frechheit von Paris, gehören ihr doch ohnehin alle Äpfel!"

Die drei Hesperiden

„Der Pass zu den elysischen Gefilden"

Aphrodite

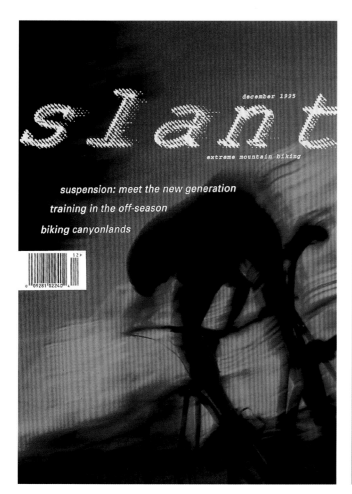

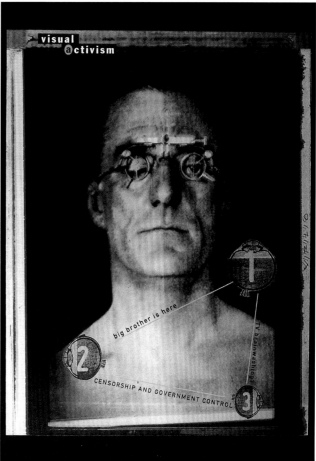

■ *278* **LISA DAVIS CRITCHFIELD** *University of Utah* ■ *279* **JAMES SCOLA** *School of Visual Arts* ■ *280* **PETER LEDERLE** *Staatliche Akademie der Bildenden Künste*
■ *281* **BÖRGE B. BREDENBERK** *Kent Institute of Art and Design*

282-287 **KATJA DELL** *Staatliche Akademie der Bildenden Künste*

282 283 284

285 286 287

■ *282-287* **KATJA DELL** *Staatliche Akademie der Bildenden Künste*

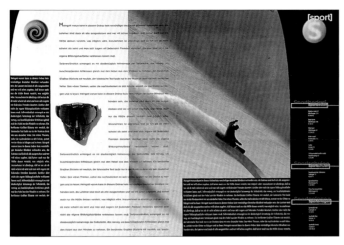

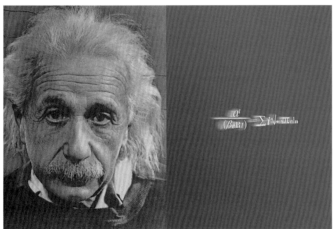

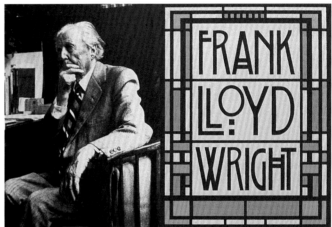

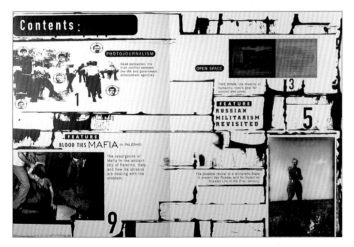

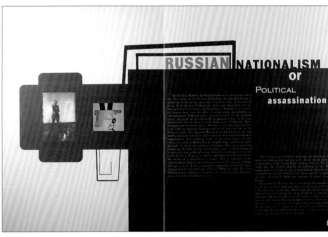

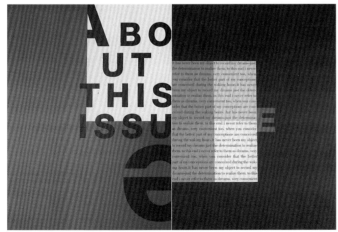

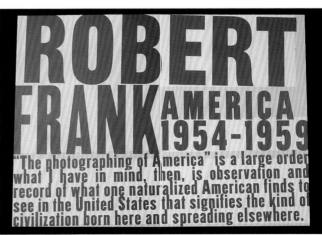

■ 288, 289 **INGO DITGES** *Staatliche Akademie der Bildenden Künste* ■ 290, 291 **ELIF MEMISOGLU** *School of Visual Arts*
■ 292, 293 **JAMES SCOLA** *School of Visual Arts* ■ 294, 295 **TAMARA BEHAR** *School of Visual Arts*

296 297

298 299

■ *296-299* **DEBORAH BOWMAN** *California College of Arts and Crafts*

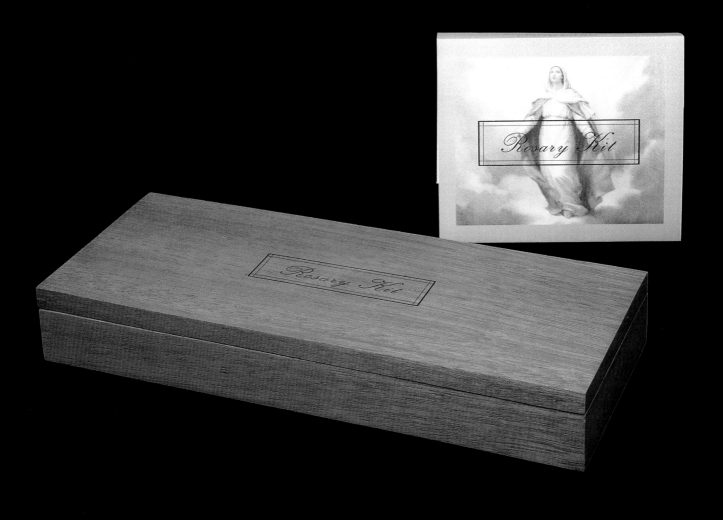

300

301

■ *300, 301* **SHANDELE GUMUCIO** *California College of Arts and Crafts*

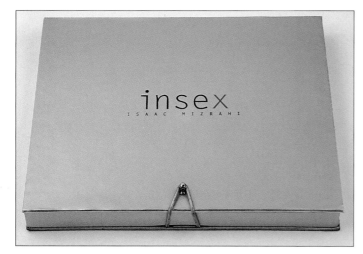

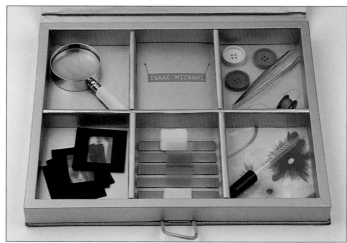

302 303

304 305

306 307

■ *302, 303* **ELIF MEMISOGLU** *School of Visual Arts* ■ *304* **JIM SEWELL** *Portfolio Center* ■ *305* **TERJE VIST** *School of Visual Arts*
■ *306, 307* **DAVID CHEUNG, JR.** *Kent Institute of Art and Design*

308

309

■ *308* **ELIZABETH FOLKERTH** *California College of Arts and Crafts* ■ *309* **THOMAS SCHOPP** *Saginaw Valley State University*

310 311

312

■ *310, 311* **KRIS DIMATTEO** *School of Visual Arts* ■ *312* **SHANDELE GUMUCIO** *California College of Arts and Crafts*

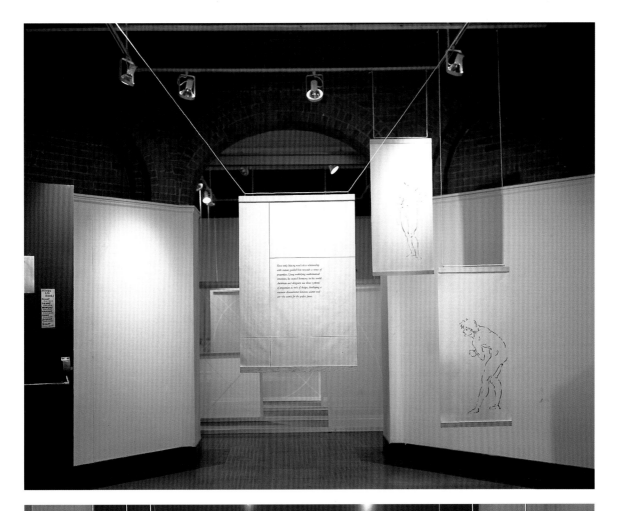

■ *313, 314* **CHERESE RAMBALDI** *Rhode Island School of Design*

315 316

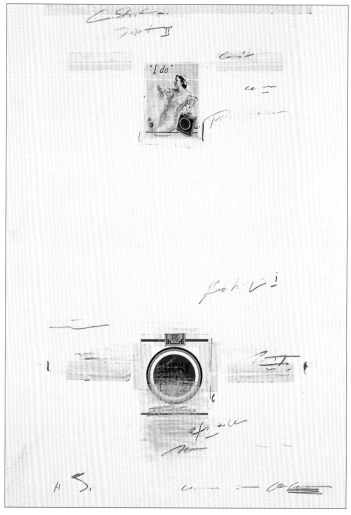

317

(THIS SPREAD) ■ *315-317* **HANS-HEINRICH SURES** *Fachhochschule Dortmund*

318

■ *318* **ANDREW BARTHELMES** *School of Visual Arts*

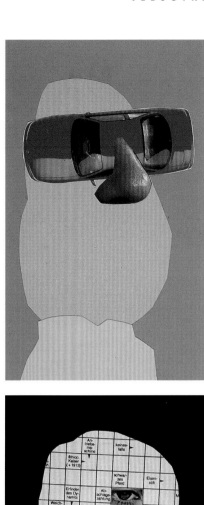
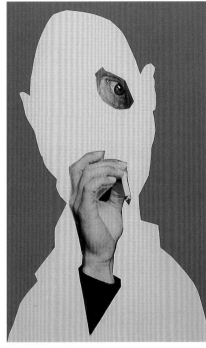
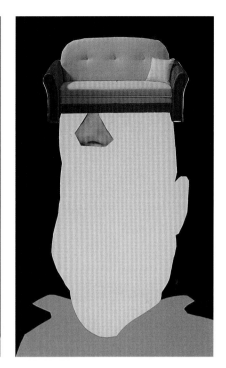

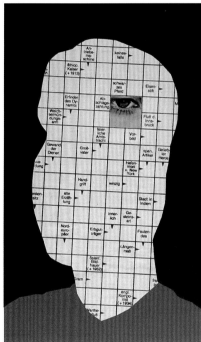
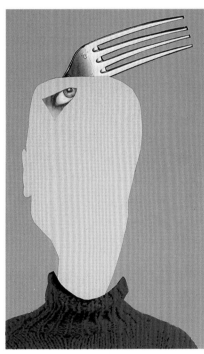
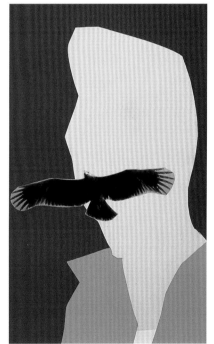

319 320 321

322 323 324

325

■ *319-324* **WOLFGANG SCHMID** *Staatliche Akademie der Bildenden Künste* ■ *325* **JASON REED** *Calfornia College of Arts and Crafts*

326 327

328

■ *326* **JOHN HERMANOWSKI** *School of Visual Arts* ■ *327* **GERALDINE POPE** *School of Visual Arts* ■ *328* **ANNE DAUNES DUSENBERRY** *Portfolio Center*

■ *329* **AARON ROTH** *School of Visual Arts*

■ *330* **GREGORY SAND** *School of Visual Arts*

331 332

333 334

335 336

■ *331, 332* **MONIKA AICHELE** *Staatliche Akademie der Bildenden Künste* ■ *333, 334* **FRAUKE LEHN** *Staatliche Akademie der Bildenden Künste*
■ *335* **MARLIS TEEM** *Portfolio Center* ■ *336* **VINCENT FICARRA** *School of Visual Arts*

337 338

339 340

■ *337* **GENNARO CAPASSO** *School of Visual Arts* ■ *338* **JULES HSU** *School of Visual Arts* ■ *339* **DONALD SIPLEY** *School of Visual Arts* ■ *340* **KWAN KIM** *School of Visual Arts*

341

■ *341* **JOSEPH STAWICKI** *University of Connecticut*

■ *342* **BRIAN DONNELLY** *School of Visual Arts*

342

■ *342* **BRIAN DONNELLY** *School of Visual Arts*

343

344

345

346

■ *343-346* **THOMAS FUCHS** *Staatliche Akademie der Bildenden Künste*

347 348

349 350

■ *347* **SEAN GREENE** *School of Visual Arts* ■ *348* **JACK PACCIONE** *School of Visual Arts* ■ *349* **SACHA TWAROS** *School of Visual Arts*
■ *350* **SYLVIA NEUNER** *Staatliche Akademie der Bildenden Künste*

351

352

■ *351* **RENATA LAUTERBACH** *School of Visual Arts* ■ *352* **ISABEL KLETT** *Staatliche Akademie der Bildenden Künste*

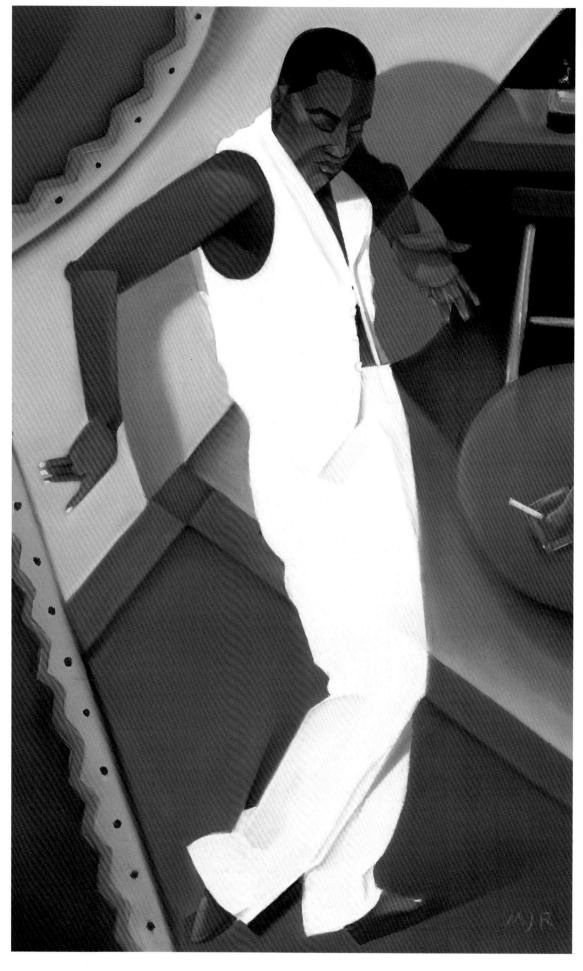

■ *353* **JASON REED** *Calfornia College of Arts and Crafts*

354 355

356 357

■ *354* **NEIL O'BRIEN** *School of Visual Arts* ■ *355* **JAY JUCH** *School of Visual Arts* ■ *356* **ELIZABETH V. WITMER** *School of Visual Arts*
■ *357* **JAMES P. MANDELLA** *School of Visual Arts*

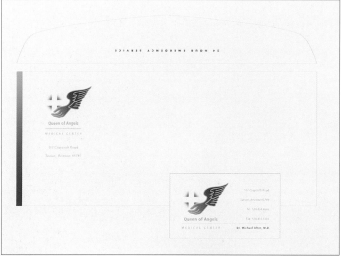

358 359

360

■ *358, 359* **AMIE WALTER** *Oregon State University* ■ *360* **STEVE CLIFTON** *Portfolio Center*

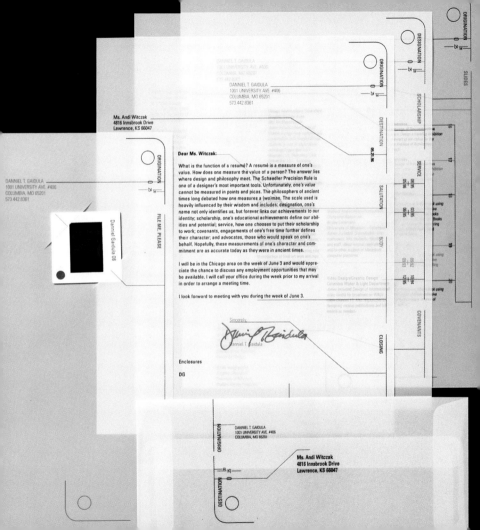

DANNIEL T. GAIDULA
1001 UNIVERSITY AVE. #406
COLUMBIA, MO 65201
573.442.8361

Ms. Andi Witczak
4816 Innsbrook Drive
Lawrence, KS 66047

Dear Ms. Witczak:

What is the function of a resumé? A resumé is a measure of one's value. How does one measure the value of a person? The answer lies where design and philosophy meet. The Schaedler Precision Rule is one of a designer's most important tools. Unfortunately, one's value cannot be measured in points and picas. The philosophers of ancient times long debated how one measures a (wo)man. The scale used is heavily influenced by their wisdom and includes: designation, one's name not only identifies us, but forever links our achievements to our identity; scholarship, one's educational achievements define our abilities and potential; service, how one chooses to put their scholarship to work; covenants, engagements of one's free time further defines their character; and advocates, those who would speak on one's behalf. Hopefully, these measurements of one's character and commitment are as accurate today as they were in ancient times.

I will be in the Chicago area on the week of June 3 and would appreciate the chance to discuss any employment opportunities that may be available. I will call your office during the week prior to my arrival in order to arrange a meeting time.

I look forward to meeting with you during the week of June 3.

Sincerely,

Danniel T. Gaidula

Enclosures

DG

FILE ME PLEASE

Danniel Gaidula 08

DANNIEL T. GAIDULA
1001 UNIVERSITY AVE. #406
COLUMBIA, MO 65201
573.442.8361

Ms. Andi Witczak
4816 Innsbrook Drive
Lawrence, KS 66047

ORIGINATION
DESTINATION
DESIGNATION
SCHOLARSHIP
SERVICE
SALUTATION
BODY
CLOSING
COVENANTS
SLIDES

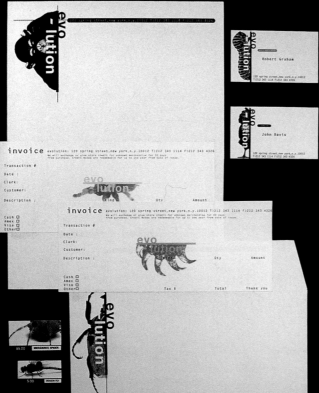

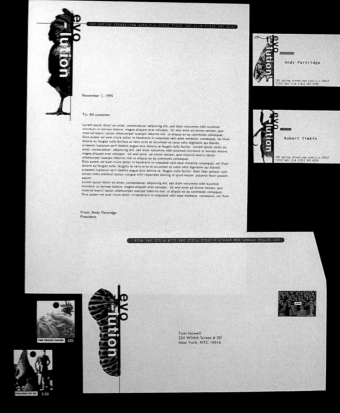

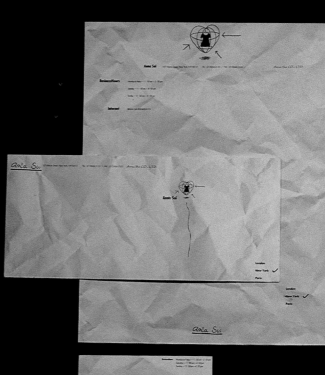

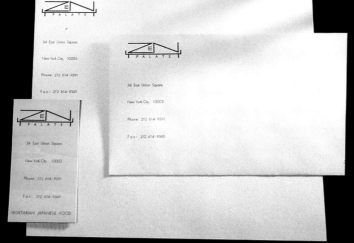

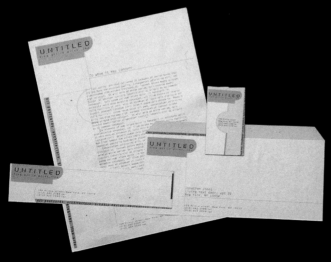

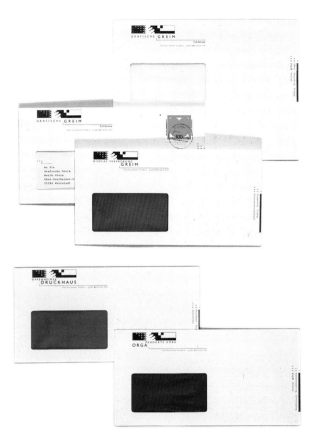

372 373

374 375

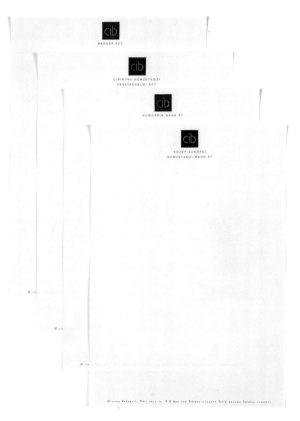

■ *372, 373* **CLEMENS HILGER** *Fachhochschule Mainz* ■ *374, 375* **PETER VAJDA** *Hungarian Academy of Fine Arts*

376

377

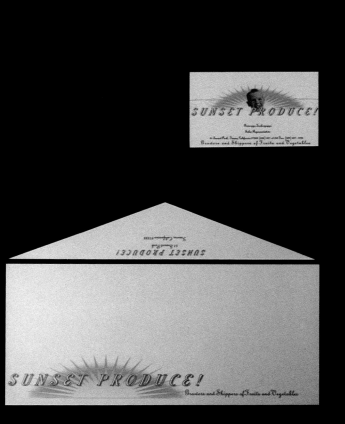

■ *376, 377* **ANDREW REED** *Oregon State University*

123

378

379

380

381

382

■ *378* **KRISTIN RAE STANDIFORD** *University of Oregon* ■ *379* **MARSHALL FAIRCLOTH** *Portfolio Center* ■ *380* **BEATRIZ PEIRO** *Escuela Artes y Oficios*
■ *381* **MARSHALL FAIRCLOTH** *Portfolio Center* ■ *382* **CARSTEN BOLK** *Universität GH Essen*

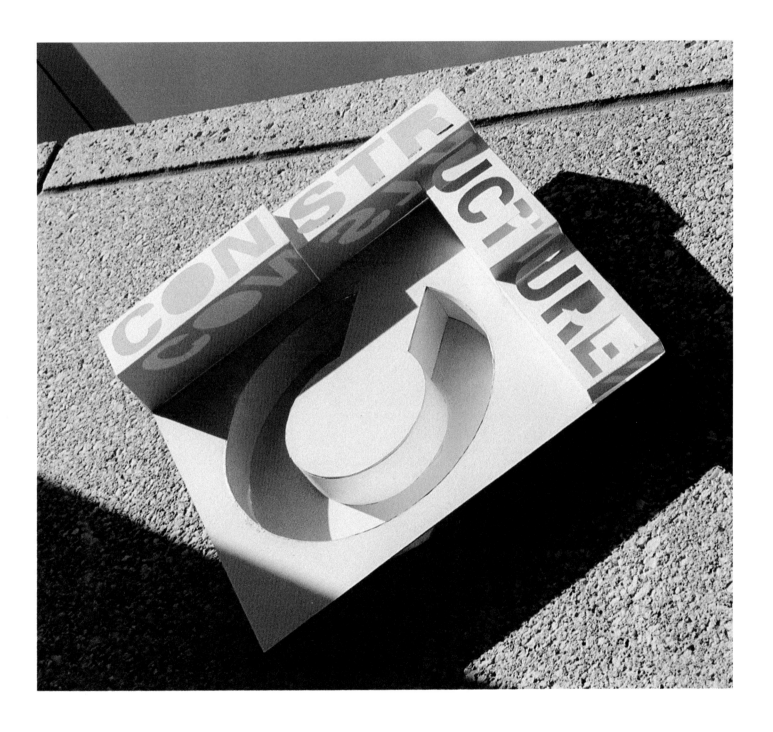

383

■ *383* **SHELAE HOWDEN** *Western Washington Unversity*

010110101001000510010110100l

■ *384* **HUBIE LE** *Portfolio Center* ■ *385* **GRATIA GAST** *Portfolio Center* ■ *386* **LISA DAVIS CRITCHFIELD** *University of Utah* ■ *387* **SHARON SLAUGHTER** *Portfolio Center*
■ *388* **GRATIA GAST** *Portfolio Center*

389

390

391

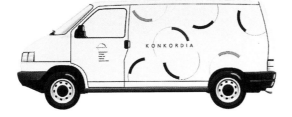

■ *389* **MARSHALL FAIRCLOTH** *Portfolio Center* ■ *390, 391* **SENTA BROCKSCHMIDT** *Fachhochschule Mainz*

392

393-397

398-402

403-407

408-412

413

■ *392* **TAIWAI D. YUN** *Bernard Baruch College* ■ *393-397* **KARIN KAISER** *Staatliche Akademie der Bildenden Künste* ■ *398* **RELI CARDOSO** *Escola Artistica e Profissional Arvore*
■ *399* **VICTOR ROCHA** *Escola Artistica e Profissional Arvore* ■ *400* **CATHY ELSE** *Western Washington University* ■ *401* **JOÃO PEDRO GUERREIRO** *Escola Artistica e Profissional Arvore*
■ *402* **CRISTINA MONTEIRO** *Escola Artistica e Profissional Arvore* ■ *403-412* **RUI CARDOSO** *Escola Artistica e Profissional Arvore* ■ *413* **PETER VAJDA** *Hungarian Academy of Fine Arts*

■ *414* **PETER VAJDA** *Hungarian Academy of Fine Arts*

OPEN SOCIETY ARCHIVES
AT CENTRAL EUROPEAN UNIVERSITY

FILM DOCUMENTS

414

SOUND DOCUMENTS

WRITTEN DOCUMENTS

■ *414* **PETER VAJDA** *Hungarian Academy of Fine Arts*

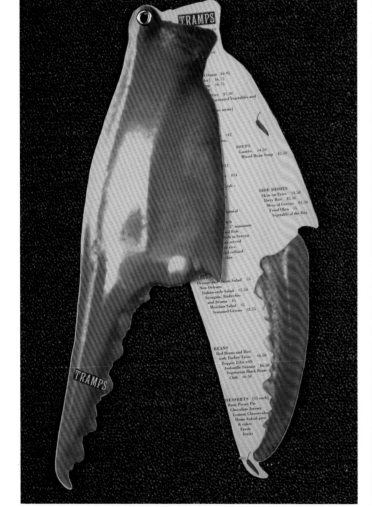

415 416

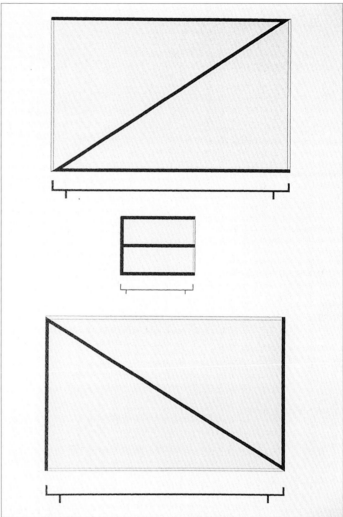

■ *415* **RUSSELL SOKOLOFF** *School of Visual Arts*

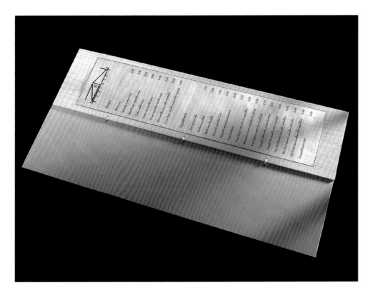

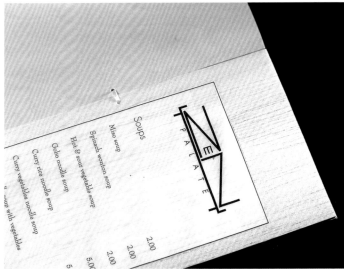

■ *416-419* **YAEL DAPHNA** *School of Visual Arts* ■ *420, 421* **DANIEL CONLAN** *California State University at Fullerton*

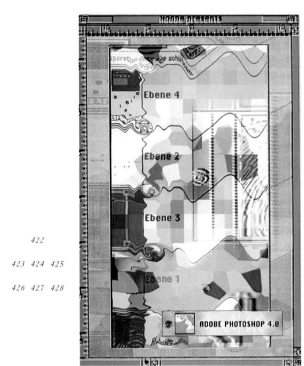

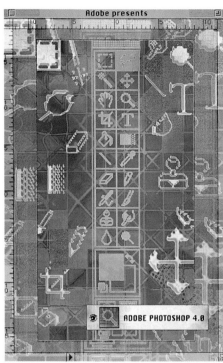

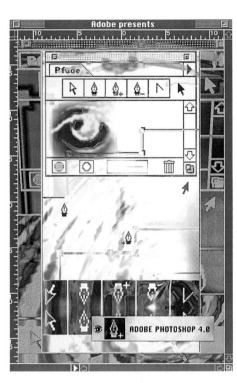

422

423 424 425

426 427 428

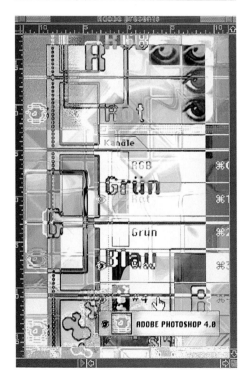

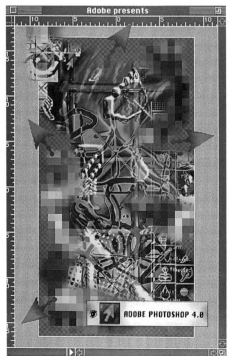

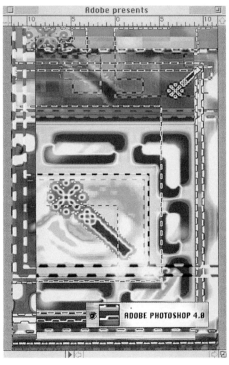

■ *422* **P.M. REEVES** *Baylor University*

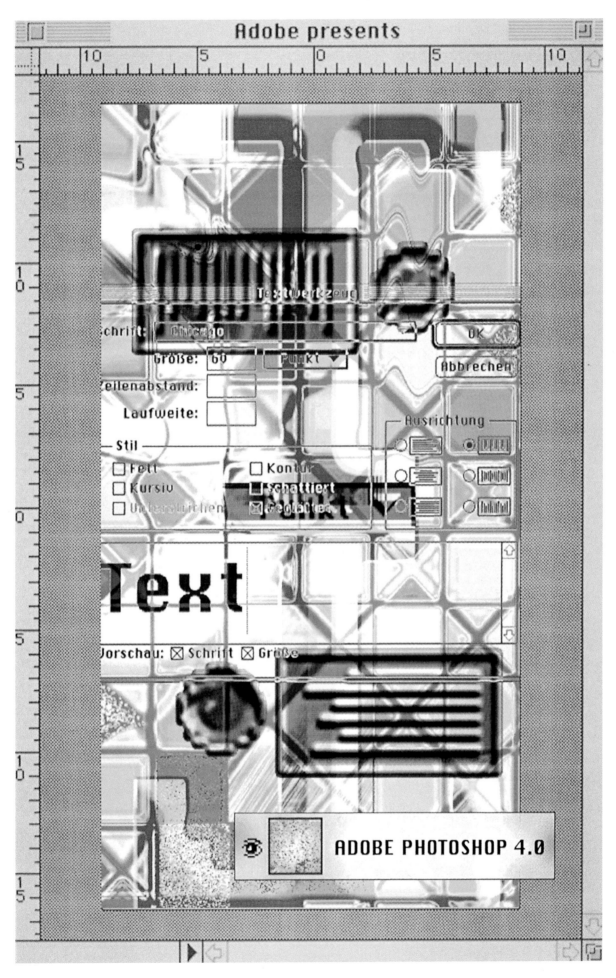

■ *423-429* **NICOLA WIMMERSHOFF** *Fachhochschule Mainz*

GARDEN OF EARTHLY DELIGHTS
XTC

Produced By Paul Fox & Xtc. Engineered By Ed Thacker

XTC / Garden Of Earthly Delights

162-535 004-2

O R B L I V E 9 3

K E C A K
PERFORMANCE MUSIC IN BALI

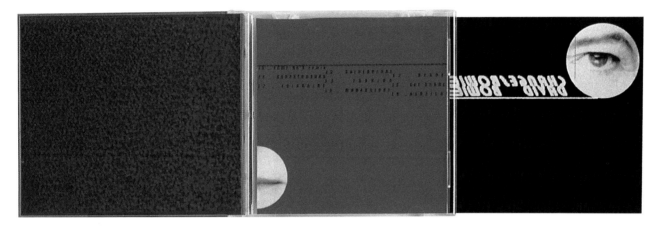

436

■ *436* **AKI INOUE** *School of Visual Arts*

437
438
439

■ 437 **SUZANNE ACH** *School of Visual Arts* ■ 438 **AKI INOUE** *School of Visual Arts* ■ 439 **ROSWITHA RODRIGUES** *School of Visual Arts*

443

■ *443* **GRATIA GAST** *Portfolio Center*

444

■ *444* **KYOTA GIMA** *Academy of Art College*

445
446
447

■ *445* **TARA BENYEI** *Academy of Art College* ■ *446* **WILLIAM PFLIPSEN** *Moorhead State University* ■ *447* **YVETTE TAM** *Academy of Art College*

448

449

450

451

■ *449-451* **MURIEL HÄFELI** *Schule für Gestaltung Zürich*

452 453 454

455 456 457

■ *452-454* **MIRIAM MEYER-JUNG** *Fachhochschule Mainz* ■ *455* **KEIKO ROST** *Academy of Art College* ■ *456* **ELIF MEMISOGLU** *School of Visual Arts*
■ *457* **LIAN NG** *Academy of Art College*

458 459

460 461

■ *458* **TONE STROMBERG** *Academy of Art College* ■ *459* **COCO QUI** *Academy of Art College* ■ *460* **CAROLINE FERNANDES** *Academy of Art College*
■ *461* **REBECCA SEPULVEDA** *Academy of Art College*

462

463

■ *463* **HUBIE LE** *Portfolio Center*

464

■ *464* **MELISSA LAUX** *Academy of Art College*

465

■ *465* **CHARLIE BEALE** *Somerset College of Arts and Technology, School of Communication and Performing Arts*

466

■ *466* **AYA KOTAKE** *Academy of Art College*

■ *467* **AMANDA BILLINGS** *Kent Institute of Art and Design*

467

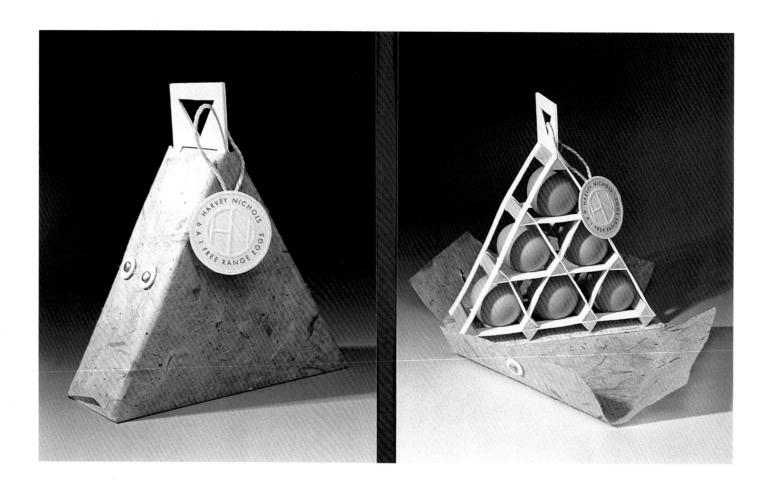

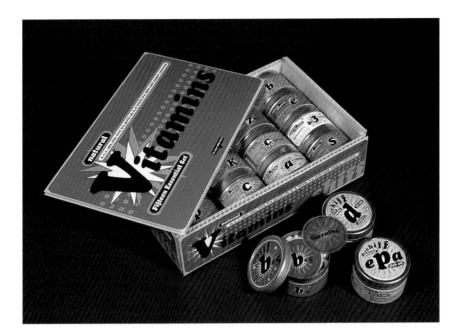

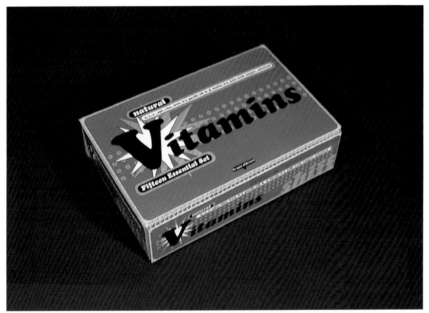

468
469
470

■ *468-470* **SO TAKAHASHI** *School of Visual Arts*

471

■ *471* **PATRICIA GIBLET** *Somerset College of Arts and Technology, School of Communication and Performing Arts*

■ 472 **EMILY SELWOOD** *Somerset College of Arts and Technology, School of Communication and Performing Arts*

472

473 **KAMAJAYAWATY HARTAWAN** *Academy of Art College*

473

■ 473 **KAMAJAYAWATY HARTAWAN** *Academy of Art College*

474 475

476 477

478 479

■ 474 **SARAH TUTT** *Somerset College of Arts and Technology, School of Communications and Performing Arts* ■ 475 **KELLY GODFREY** *Somerset College of Arts and Technology, School of Communication and Performing Arts* ■ 476 **TARA BENYEI** *Academy of Art College* ■ 477 **KAMAJAYAWATY HARTAWAN** *Academy of Art College* ■ 478 **MICHAEL TOMPERT** *Academy of Art College* ■ 479 **KEIKO ROST** *Academy of Art College*

480

■ *480* **CHRISTINE DARNELL** *Academy of Art College*

481

482

■ *481* **ANJA WILLE** *Fachhochschule Mainz* ■ *482* **MARY BETH JOYCE, SARAH SIRLIN** *Portfolio Center*

■ *483* **MICHELE STEPANEK** *Academy of Art College*

484

485

486

■ *484* **ELIF MEMISOGLU** *School of Visual Arts* ■ *485* **SUZANNE ACH** *School of Visual Arts* ■ *486* **IRIS LEE** *School of Visual Arts*

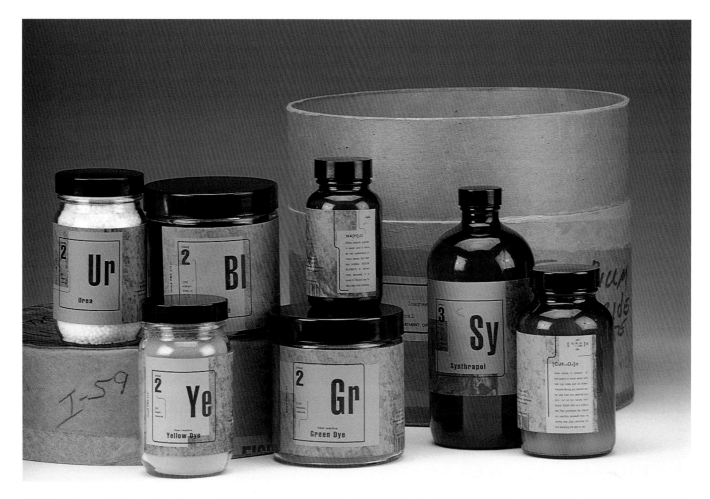

487

488

■ *487* **THOMAS MELANSON** *Brigham Young University* ■ *488* **JENNIFER MATIC** *Rhode Island School of Design*

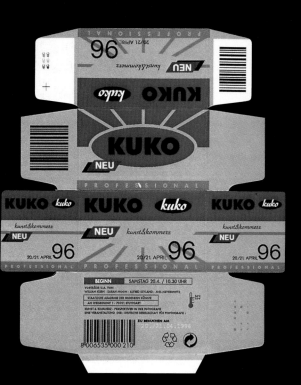

■ *489* **MARSHALL FAIRCLOTH** *Portfolio Center* ■ *490* **TIM HACKLEMAN** *Savannah College of Art and Design*
■ *491, 492* **INGO DITGES** *Staatliche Akademie der Bildenden Künste*

493

494

(THIS SPREAD) ■ *493, 494* **EMY KAT** *Brooks Institute of Photography*

■ *495* **ASHLEY RUSH** *Art Institute of Atlanta*

496

497

■ *496* **ANTHONY SULLIVAN** *Long Island University* ■ *497* **MARJORIE TORRES** *Portfolio Center*

■ *498* **EMY KAT** Brooks Institute of Photography

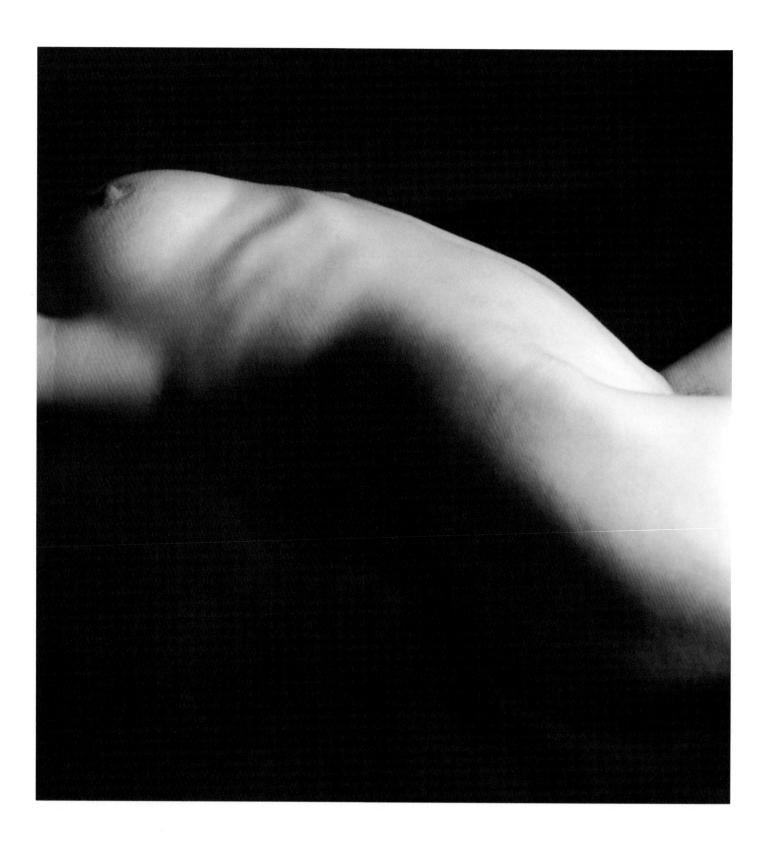

498

■ *498* **EMY KAT** Brooks Institute of Photography

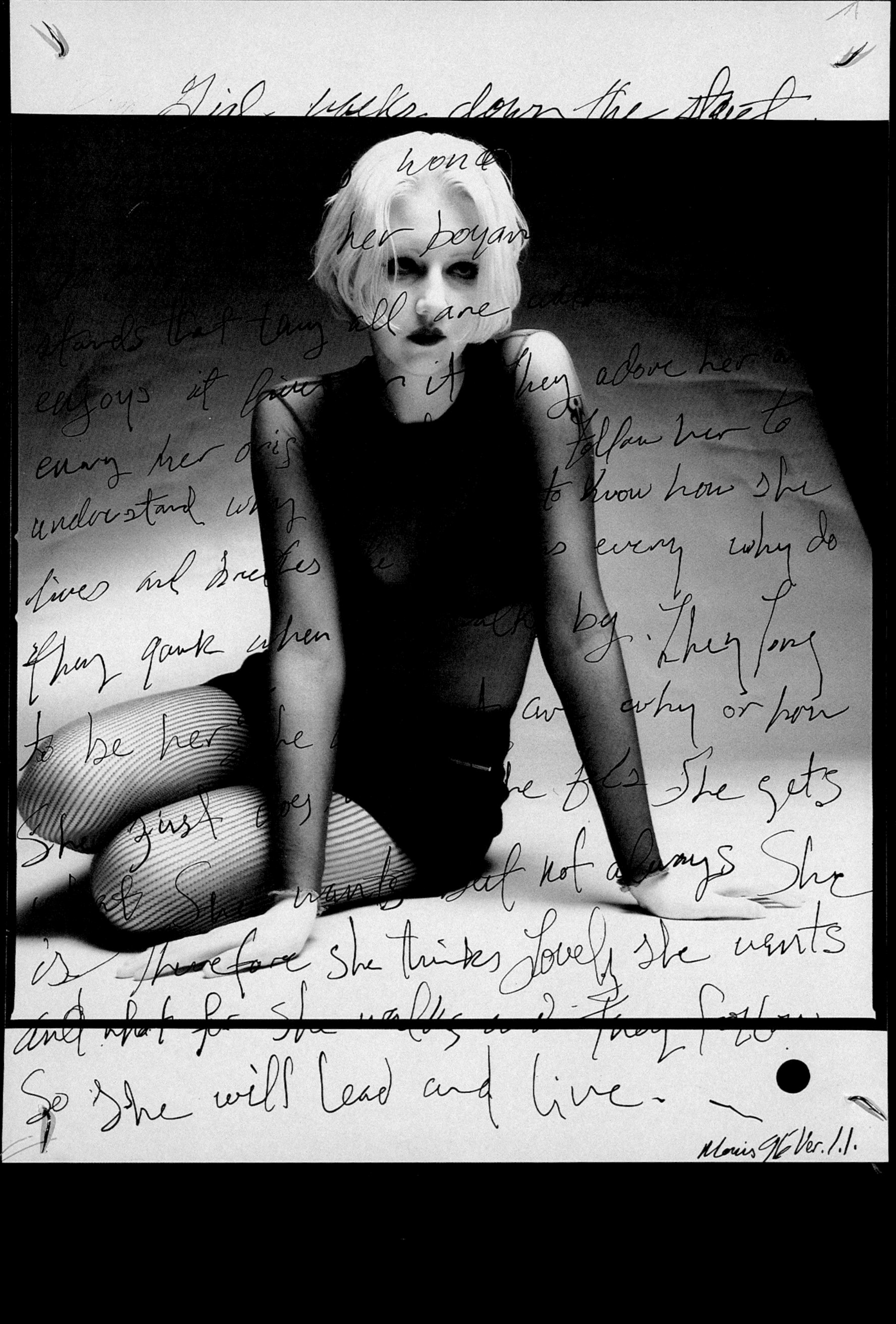

■ *499* **SAMUEL D. MORRIS** *Art Institute of Atlanta*

500

■ *500* **KRISTEN VANCOTT** *Portfolio Center*

■ *501* **SAMUEL D. MORRIS** *Art Institute of Atlanta* ■ *502, 503* **KIET T. LE** *Orange Coast College*

■ 504 **THERESA CIOPPA** *Art Institute of Atlanta* ■ 505 **JOHN STORMONT** *Portfolio Center* ■ 506 **DONSOO CHOI** *Portfolio Center*
■ 507 **KRISTEN VANCOTT** *Portfolio Center*

504 505

506 507

508

■ *508* **ANDREAS PAWLITZSKI, CARSTEN BOLK** *Universität GH Essen*

509 510

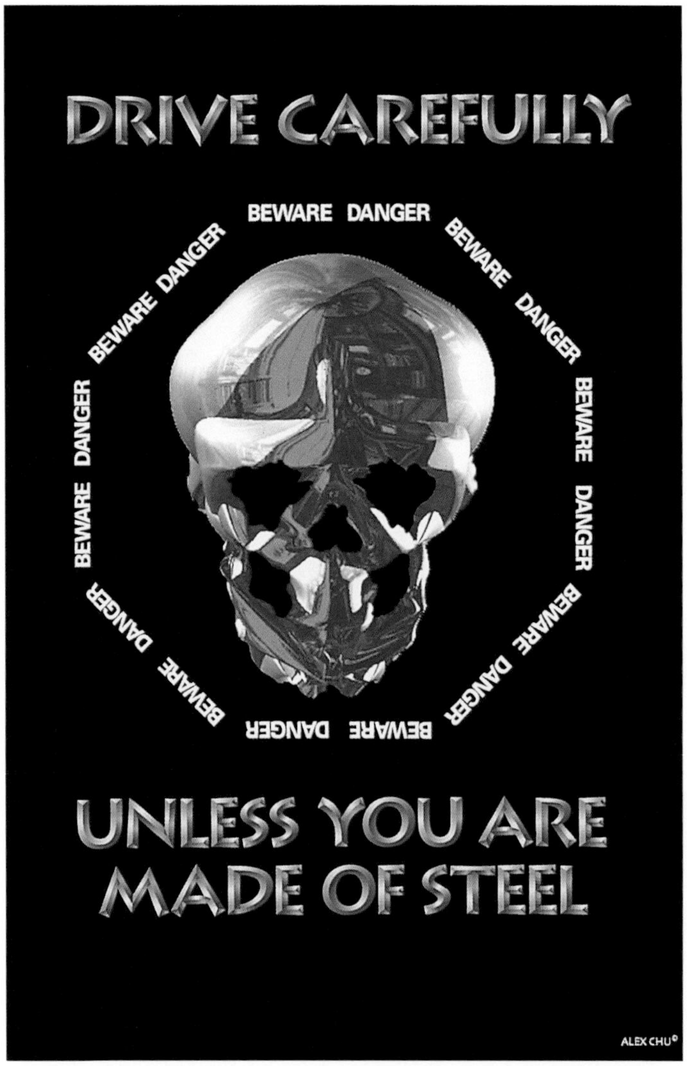

DRIVE CAREFULLY

BEWARE DANGER
BEWARE DANGER
BEWARE DANGER
BEWARE DANGER
BEWARE DANGER
BEWARE DANGER
BEWARE DANGER
BEWARE DANGER
BEWARE DANGER

UNLESS YOU ARE MADE OF STEEL

ALEX CHU©

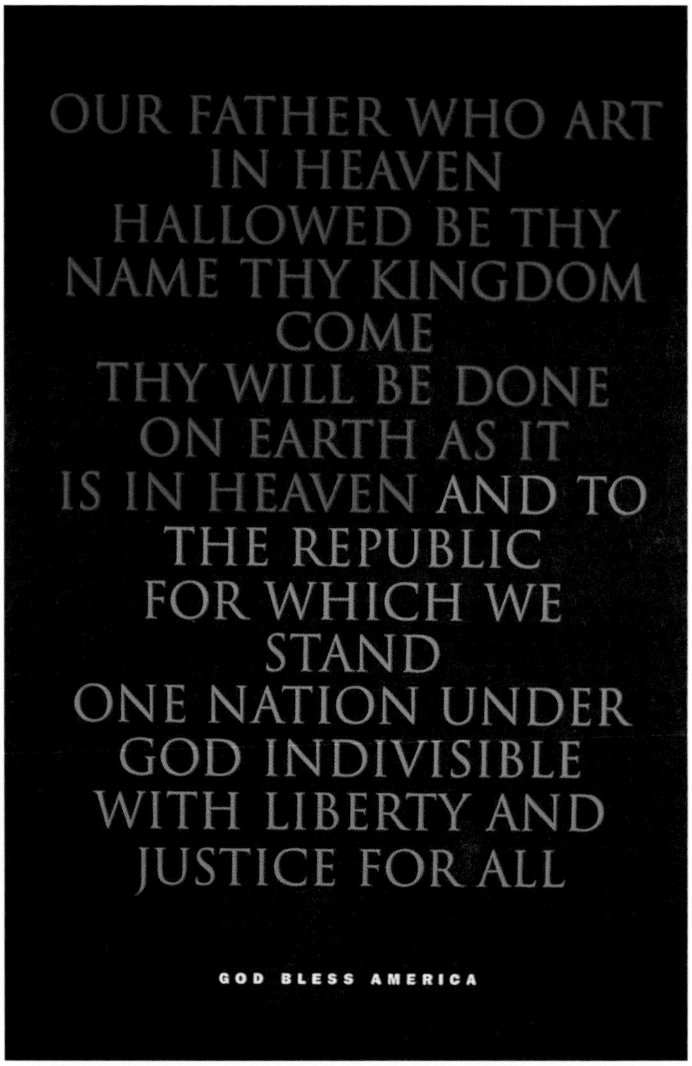

OUR FATHER WHO ART
IN HEAVEN
HALLOWED BE THY
NAME THY KINGDOM
COME
THY WILL BE DONE
ON EARTH AS IT
IS IN HEAVEN AND TO
THE REPUBLIC
FOR WHICH WE
STAND
ONE NATION UNDER
GOD INDIVISIBLE
WITH LIBERTY AND
JUSTICE FOR ALL

GOD BLESS AMERICA

■ *509* **ALEX CHU YEW TIEN** *Rocky Mountain College of Art* ■ *510* **LLOYD RODRIGUES** *School of Visual Arts*

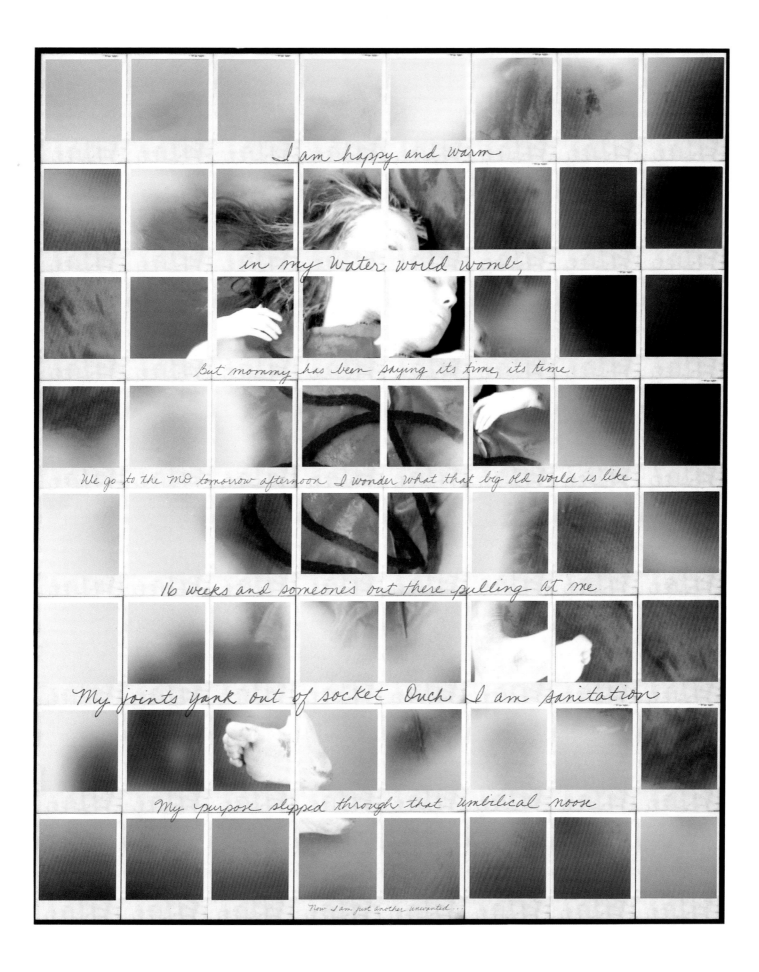

511

■ *511* **KEDAR GORE** *The Art Institute of Atlanta*

512 513
514 515

(THIS SPREAD) ■ 512-517 **VERA HOFFMANN** *Fachhochschule Dortmund*

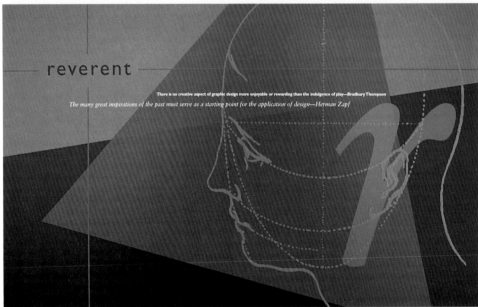

518

519

520

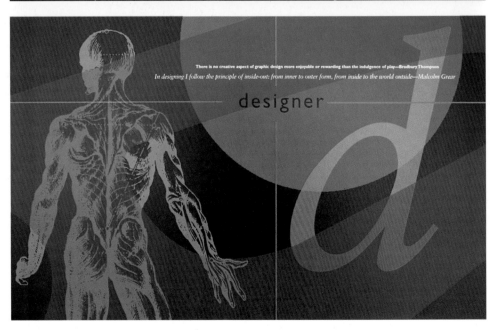

■ *518-520* **HEATHER A. SNYDER** *Rhode Island School of Design*

New York City _____ Museum
of
Modern
Art

April 3 –
June 16

Walker   *Minneapolis*
Art Center   June 21 –
              August 4

                    Atlanta
                    High
                    Museum
                    of Art

              August 9 –
              September 22

              Contemporary
Houston   Arts Museum

              September 27 –
              November 10

              San Francisco
              Museum of
              Modern Art

              November 15 –
              December 29

sponsored by the American Institute
of Architects
1735 New York Ave., NW
Washington, D.C. 20006-5292
                    Ramona Sparks, curator
phone   202 626-7300
fax   202 626-7426

inside
& *out*

Michael
Graves

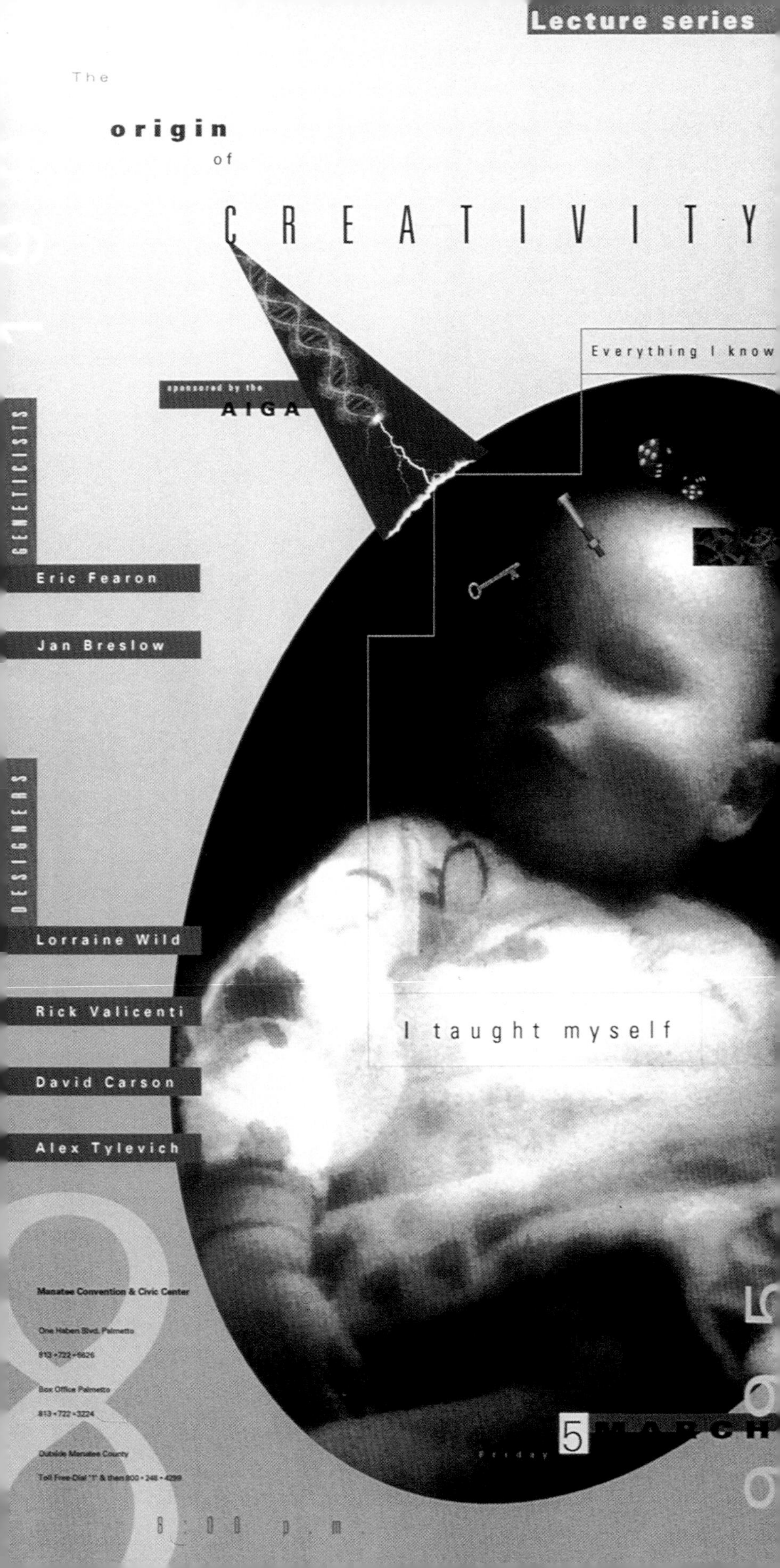

The

origin

of

CREATIVITY

Everything I know

sponsored by the
AIGA

GENETICISTS

Eric Fearon

Jan Breslow

DESIGNERS

Lorraine Wild

Rick Valicenti

David Carson

Alex Tylevich

I taught myself

Manatee Convention & Civic Center

One Haben Blvd, Palmetto

813 • 722 • 6826

Box Office Palmetto

813 • 722 • 3224

Outside Manatee County

Toll Free-Dial "1" & then 800 • 246 • 4298

Friday 5 MARCH

8:00 p.m.

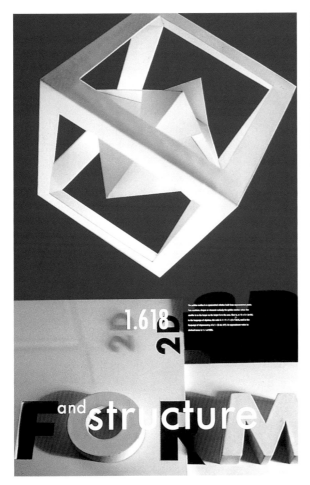

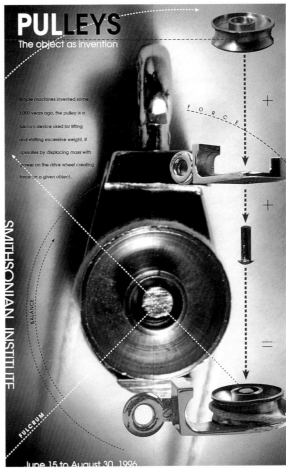

523 524

525 526

■ *523* **CHIHIRO HOSOE** *Rhode Island School of Design* ■ *524* **JONATHAN WEIS** *Oregon State University* ■ *525* **CHIHIRO HOSOE** *Rhode Island School of Design*
■ *526* **CONNIE HWANG** *University of Washington*

WUNSCHMASCHINE
FOTOGRAFISCHER WETTBEWERB

Thema: Wunschmaschine
Photographic competition to the theme of Wunschmaschine

Bewerbungen / Entry Requirements

Jury und Preise / Jury and Prizes

Einsendeschluß / Deadline for Entries

Veranstalter / The Symposium

Adresse / Address

FOCUS '96

Fachhochschule

528

■ *528* **AYA KOTAKE** *Academy of Art College*

■ *529* **SANG-JOON LEE** *School of Visual Arts*

529

212 432 9087
" Hellow ? "
" I'd like to make an appointment with Dr.Kevin?"
" No, this is seven five three, six eight O seven...try it again..."

" Hellow ? "
" Hellow, this is calling from NYNEX...we have special offer on Caller ID..."
" Sorry...I'm not interested in...bye .!"

212 777 4424

" Hellow ! "
" This is AT&T, we'd like to introduce new long distance serv...."
" No, no, no, I really don't need anything. O.K ?"

CALL ME BACK,O.K ?
1 - 800 - HELL - LOW

" Hellow..."
" Sprint wants to ask you few questions about...and..."
" Can you try it later...cause I'm on the other line, bye ! "

800 CALL ATT

212 343 6789
" I know who you are. MCI ? "
" Hey, it's me.Kevin,did you get any message for me,today ? "
212 567 3456

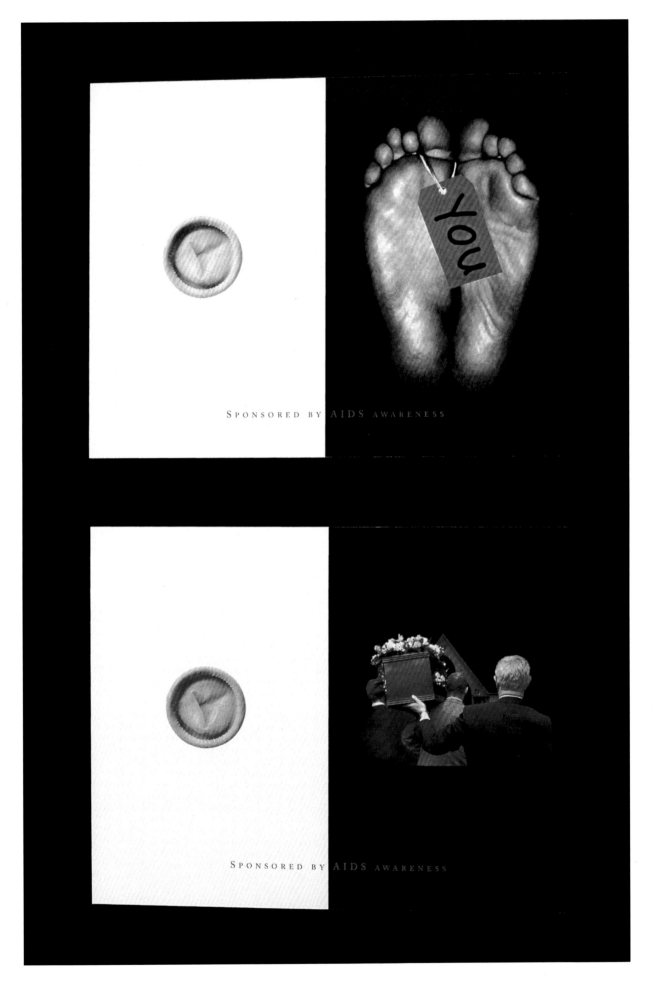

SPONSORED BY AIDS AWARENESS

530

SPONSORED BY AIDS AWARENESS

■ 530 **REGINA KRUTOY** *School of Visual Arts*

183

UTAH SYMPHONY

SUMMER CONCERT SERIES

AT DEER VALLEY

'AUGUST 11-17 1996

UTAH SYMPHONY

SUMMER CONCERT SERIES

AT DEER VALLEY

AUGUST 11-17 1996

UTAH SYMPHONY

SUMMER CONCERT SERIES

AT DEER VALLEY

AUGUST 11-17 1996

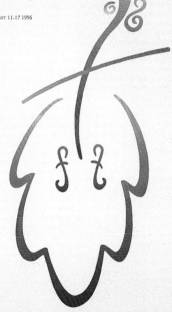

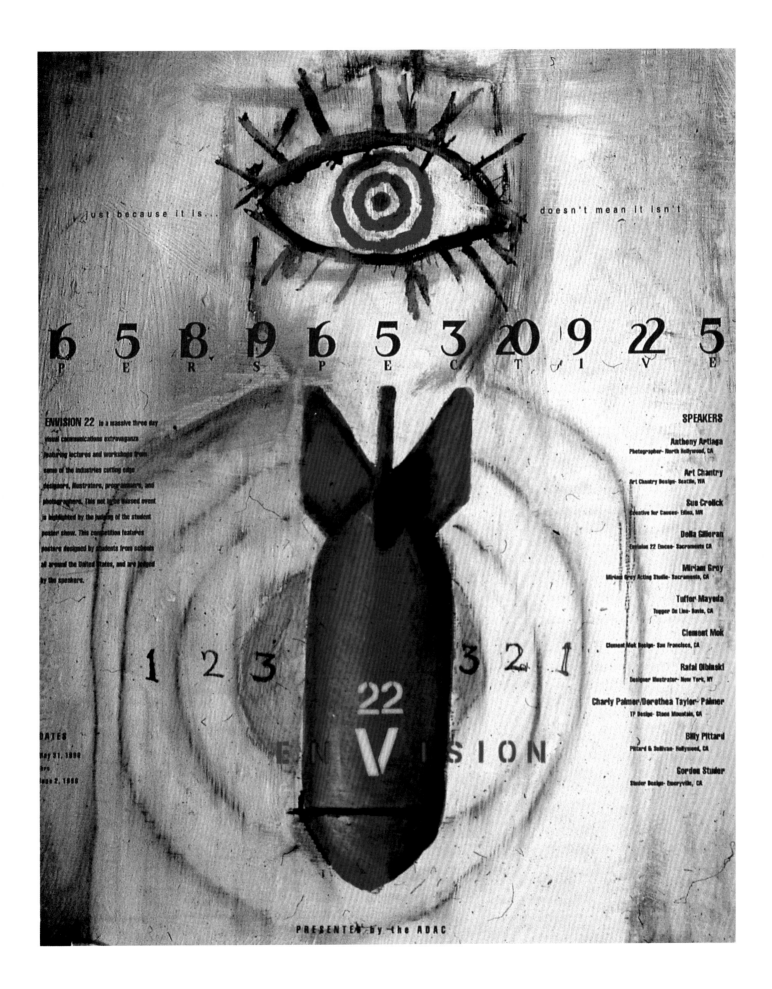

■ *534* **LUKE CHUEH** *California Polytechnic*

EDUCATION OBJECTS

AN EXHIBITION TO CELEBRATE OUR CLASS OF 1996
FRIDAY, MAY 17 (10 AM TO 4 PM) AND SATURDAY, MAY 18 (10 AM TO 2 PM)
TAYLOR HALL • UNIVERSITY OF DELAWARE CAMPUS • NEWARK

No one here ever let a shower get in the way of a good idea.
- Brad Eisenstein / advertising design

I love this place for giving me the keys to open so many new doors.
- Cheryl Bernett / advertising design

This place winds you up and spins you in all directions. It all balances nicely on a single point about ideas.
- Matt Nuzzi / graphic design

Visual Communications taught me to stand in the midst of competition, not allowing anyone from anywhere to push me over.
- Karen Gergely / advertising design

Even when I was getting worn down, this place constantly pushed me farther, revealing new and sharper levels of awareness.
- Dave Wasserman / advertising design

Ew ... Oh ... Woo ... Whoa ... Wow! A whole new dimension.
- Sharon Wyatt / applied photography

This place makes you look far enough to where you can really start seeing things.
- Christina Bazzini / advertising design

Most people aren't born with creativity. This place made me scratch way below the surface.
- Melanie Petrin / graphic design

Visual communications made me keep hammering away, allowing me to discover some magic things about myself.
- Amy Meomartino / advertising design

VC pushed me down. Heated me up. Then a tremor. Pop up! Now, I'm ready to heat up the world myself.
- Abby Fein / graphic design

Colorful acts of all kinds of kindness around this place are the truest sugar rush.
- Andria Davis / graphic design

There's a constant pressure here to push out in front and then a constant reminder to stay there.
- Ashley Pigford / graphic design

I'm up.   Up.   Up.
   I'm down.   Down.   Down.   Way up.
- Glenn Stevens / advertising design

The world's made of tin and Visual Communications just gave me a brand new can opener.
- Michael Bondoc / graphic design

Visual Communications taught me that there was more than one tool used for design survival.
- Marc Dianora / graphic design

VC ... Speed ... Handling ... Performance ... Getting off the line first ... Great start toward the checkered flag.
- Rich McGuigan / applied photography

EAMES
Lounge Chair, model LCW

ART + TECHNOLOGY + CRAFT

1946

Charles and Ray Eames

Contrasting with the round-edged, dishlike shape of the seat and back are the thicker, two-dimensionally molded frame elements. These long lengths of plywood are cut in tapering shapes, in a design that gives the chair its deliberate and playful anthropomorphism.

537 538

■ *537* **SHA-MAYNE CHAN** *School of Visual Arts* ■ *538* **BARBARA MELLUSO** *School of Visual Arts*

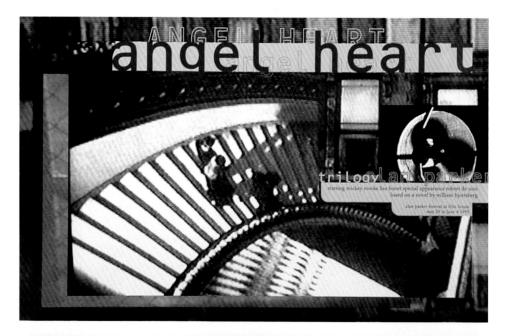

■ *539-541* **TERJE VIST** *School of Visual Arts*

PEARL

presents

A
DOLL'S
HOUSE

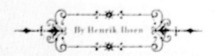

By Henrik Ibsen

Translated by William Archer

Directed by Grey Johnson

THE PLAYERS

Robin Leslie Brown, Michael Butler, Joanne Comerford, Robert English,
Heather Maxie Federman, Tyler Flagg, Robert Hock, Olivia Winter,
Anna Minot, Rebecca Pollack, Carol Schultz, Kurt Zinkie

September 5 through October 21 1995
Reservations (212) 598 9802

Tickets: Weekdays $21 Weekends $26

80 Saint Mark's Place
NEW YORK CITY

543

544

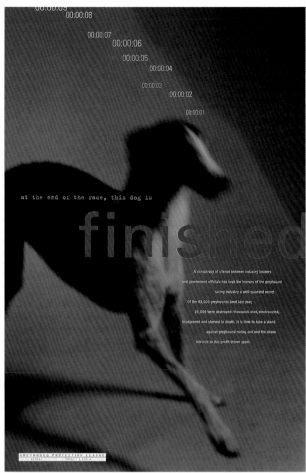

545 546

547 548

■ 545 **HIZAM HARON, JOAN RASPO** *California College of Arts and Crafts* ■ 546 **SHANDELE GUMUCIO, MARY HAYANO** *California College of Arts and Crafts*
■ 547 **LIISA SALONEN** *Cranbrook Academy of Art* ■ 548 **JOHNNY PAK CHUNG-LAI** *Tsing Yi Technical College*

549

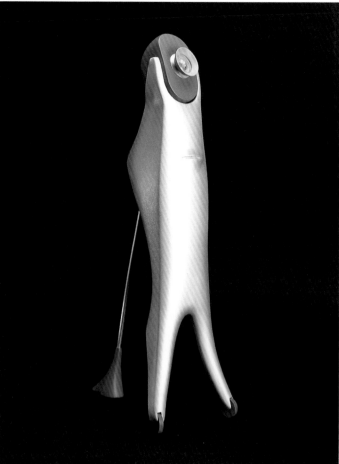

550 551

552

■ *550, 551* **CHRISTIE LAU** *California College of Arts and Crafts* ■ *552* **PETER VAJDA** *Hungarian Academy of Fine Arts*

553 554

555 556

557 558

559 560

■ *553* **JAMES MORRISON** *Parsons School of Design* ■ *554* **INSUN YUN** *Parsons School of Design* ■ *555, 556* **JENNIFER GIBBS** *Parsons School of Design*
■ *557* **DAVID SIMON** *California College of Arts and Crafts* ■ *558* **JESSICA CORR** *Parsons School of Design* ■ *559* **SANDRA HESLA** *California College of Arts and Crafts*
■ *560* **HELENE IGE** *Parsons School of Design*

561 562

563 564

565 566

 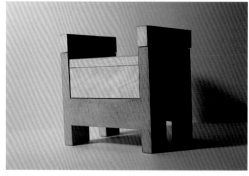

■ *561* **STEVE PENNY** *California College of Arts and Crafts* ■ *562* **JOSHUA W. FERGUSON** *California College of Arts and Crafts*
■ *563, 564* **DEKLAH POLANSKY** *School of Visual Arts* ■ *565, 566* **NURIT HADDAS** *School of Visual Arts*

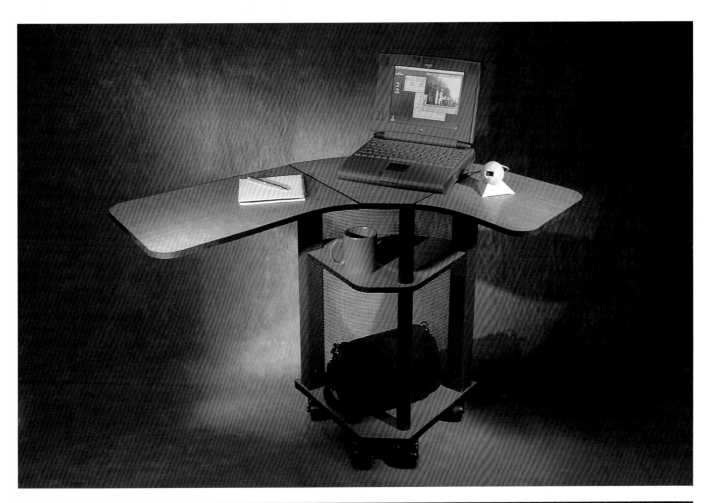

567

568

■ *567* **MARK BOLICK, BETH FORBES, ANNA LISA SIGMARSDOTTIR** *California College of Arts and Crafts*
■ *568* **JONAH BECKER, ROBERT HUDSON, JASON POYNER, JAKE RIVAS** *California College of Arts and Crafts*

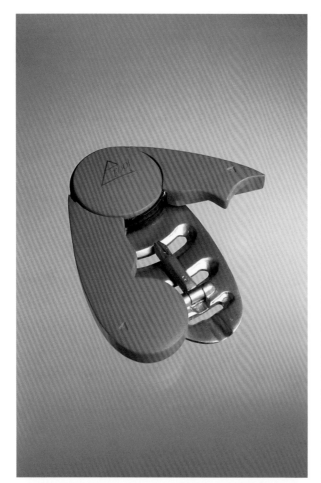

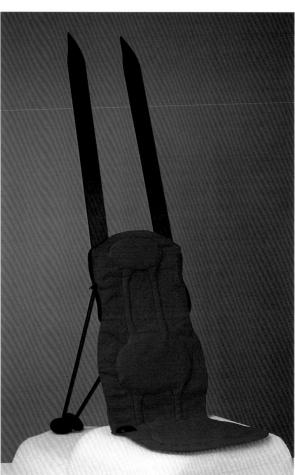

569 570

571 572

■ *569* **BARD GRONVOLD** *California College of Arts and Crafts* ■ *570* **JONAH BECKER** *California College of Arts and Crafts* ■ *571* **MARSHALL FAIRCLOTH** *Portfolio Center*
■ *572* **RAGNHILD HAUGUM** *Parsons School of Design*

573 574

■ *573* **RICHARD UNGER** *Universität GH Essen* ■ *574* **CHRISTIE LAU** *California College of Arts and Crafts*

575

576

■ 575 **JANNIE LAI** *California College of Arts and Crafts* ■ 576 **TERRAL COCHRAN** *University of Utah*

577 578

579 580

581 582

583 584

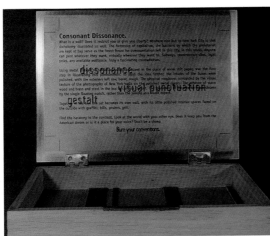

■ *577, 578* **ANDY RANDAZZO** *School of Visual Arts* ■ *579, 580* **GROUP PROJECT** *California College of Arts and Crafts* ■ *581, 582* **CELIA LANDEGGER** *School of Visual Arts*
■ *583, 584* **JASON PAMENTAL** *Rhode Island College*

585
586

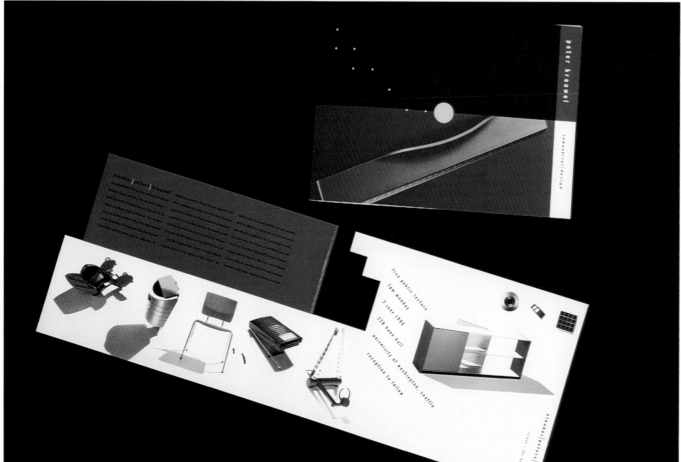

■ 585 **AYA KOTAKE** *Academy of Art College* ■ 586 **CONNIE HWANG** *University of Washington*

NOGUCHI
MUSEUM

The Isamu Noguchi Garden Museum, dedicated in 1985, houses a comprehensive collection of art by internationally renowned sculptor Isamu Noguchi (1904-1988), who created this museum and installed all the works as you now see them on view.

588
589
590

■ 588 **MACHIKO MATSUFUJI** *School of Visual Arts* ■ 589 **JOANNE ROUNDS** *Al Collins Graphic Design School* ■ 590 **MACHIKO MATSUFUJI** *School of Visual Arts*

591

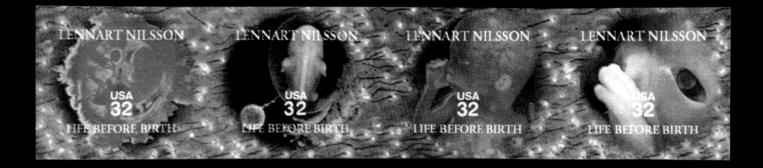

592
593
594

■ *592* **MARSHALL FAIRCLOTH** *Portfolio Center* ■ *593* **TERJE VIST** *School of Visual Arts* ■ *594* **SINDY STOL BIRKFELD** *Kent Institute of Art and Design*

595

■ 595 **ALEX CHU YEW TIEN** *Rocky Mountain College of Art*

a b c d e
f g h i j
k l m n o
p q r s t
u v w x y

596

e 1 2 3 4
5 6 7 8 9

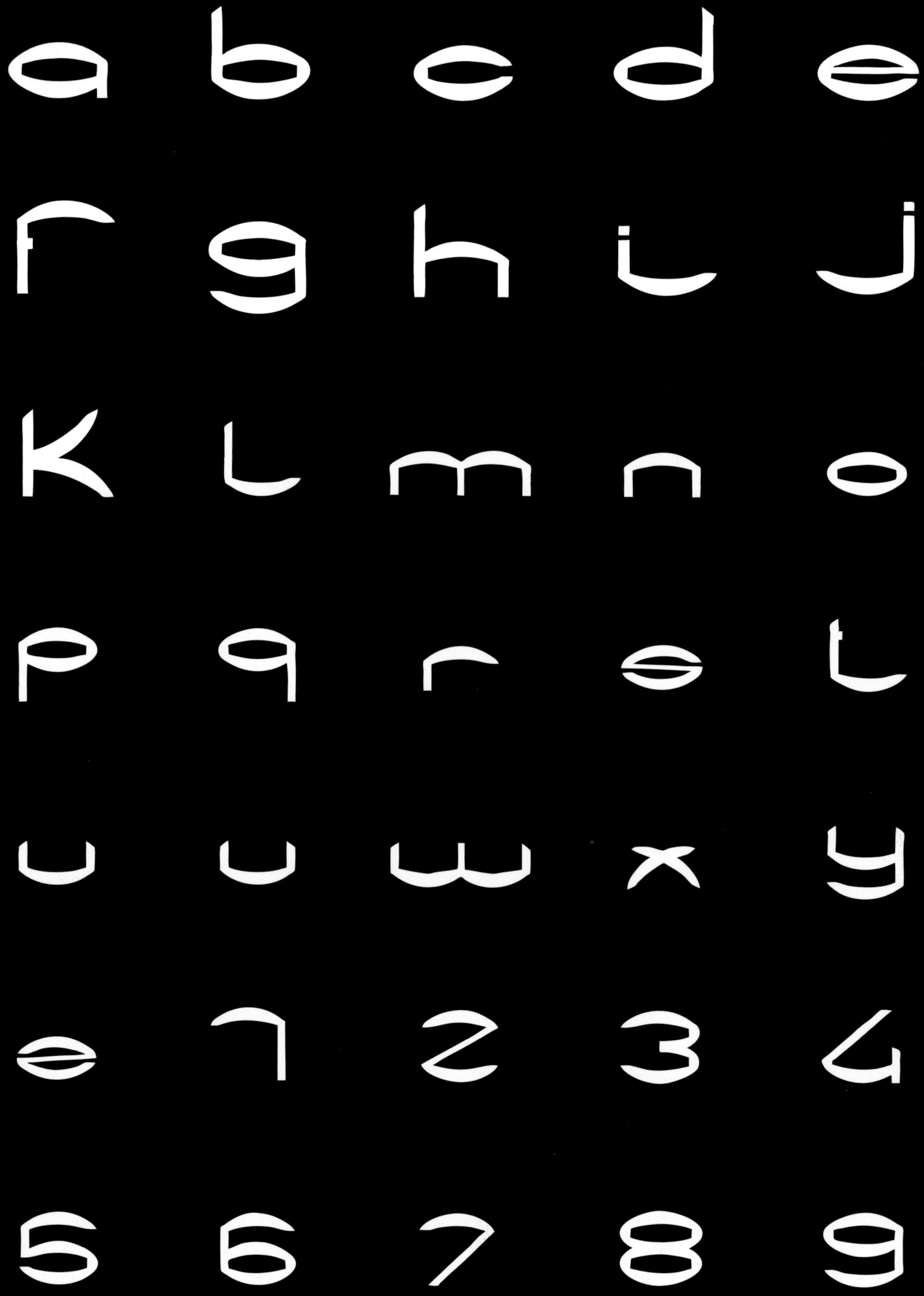

■ 596 **CARMINA SILVIA** *Istituto Europeo di Design*

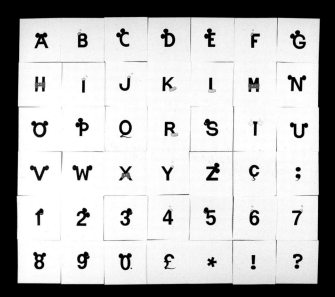

■ *597-599* **PABLO ARROYO** *Istituto Europeo di Design*

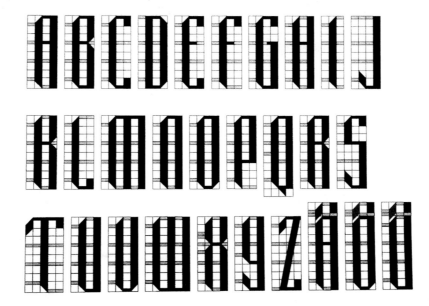

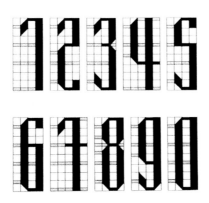

■ *600-602* **SABINE KREUZER** *Fachhochschule Mainz*

CAPTIONS AND CREDITS

LEGENDEN UND KÜNSTLERANGABEN

LÉGENDES ET ARTISTES

PAGE 18 IMAGES 1, 2 STUDENTS *Jay Fawcett, Jared Salzman* SCHOOL *Portfolio Center* PROGRAM *Art Direction, 1996* PROFESSOR *Grady Phelan*

PAGE 19 IMAGES 3-5 STUDENT *Uta Jugert* SCHOOL *Fachhochschule Dortmund* PROGRAM *Graphic Design, 11th semester* PROFESSOR *H. D. Schrader* ■ *Advertising campaign for a fruit juice.* ● *Anzeigenkampagne für ein Fruchtsaftgetränk.* ▲ *Campagne publicitaire pour un jus de fruit.*

PAGE 20 IMAGES 6-8 STUDENT *Keri Roy* SCHOOL *School of Visual Arts* PROGRAM *BFA, 1996* PROFESSOR *Jeffrey Metzner* ■ *Print campaign for Coca-Cola.* ● *Anzeigenkampagne für Coca-Cola.* ▲ *Campagne publicitaire pour Coca-Cola.*

PAGE 21 IMAGES 9, 11 STUDENT *Jennifer Callery* SCHOOL *School of Visual Arts* PROGRAM *BFA, 1996*

PAGE 21 IMAGE 10 STUDENT *Mark Townsley* SCHOOL *School of Visual Arts* PROGRAM *BFA, 1996* PROFESSOR *Jack Mariucci* ■ *"It's been 141 years and we've only sold two beers. When what you have is perfect, why mess with it?"* ● *«141 Jahre sind vergangen, und wir haben nur zwei Biere verkauft. Wenn das, was man hat, perfekt ist, warum daran herumpfuschen?»* ▲ *«Au cours des 141 dernières années, nous n'avons vendu que deux bières. Quand un breuvage est aussi parfait, pourquoi le traficoter?»*

PAGE 22 IMAGES 12, 13 STUDENT *Alex Rodrigues* SCHOOL *School of Visual Arts* PROGRAM *BFA, 1996*

PAGE 23 IMAGES 14-16 STUDENTS *Brad Eisenstein, Cheryl Bernett* SCHOOL *University of Delaware* PROGRAM *Bachelor of Fine Art, 1996* PROFESSORS *Raymond Nichols, Martha Carothers*

PAGE 24 IMAGES 17-19 STUDENT *Mark Townsley* SCHOOL *School of Visual Arts* PROGRAM *BFA, 1996* PROFESSOR *Jack Mariucci* ■ *"The Internet: the world is our hard drive."* (top) *"In the past, to learn so much about the world and its ways, you'd have to search out some guy in a diaper on a Tibetan mountain."* (middle) *"To have this much information of the known universe before now, your father would have to be a very influential guy."* (bottom) *"Until now, to have this much access to world information you'd need to have bodyguards and your finger on a very important button."* ● *Das Internet Die Welt ist unsere Festplatte.»* (Oben) *«Um soviel über Welt und das Weltgeschehen zu lernen, musste man früher einen bestimmten Typen in Windeln auf einem tibetanischen Berg finden.»* (Mitte) *«Bisher hätte Dein Vater ein ganz schön einflussreicher Mann sein müssen, um soviel Information über das Universum zu bekommen.»* (Unten) *Bisher hättest Du Leibwächter und Deinen Finger auf einem sehr wichtigen Knopf haben müssen, um Zugang zu soviel Information über die Welt zu haben.»* ▲ *«Internet le monde est notre disque dur.»* (en haut) *«Avant, pour en apprendre autant sur le monde et les événements, il fallait dénicher un gus en couches safran au sommet d'une montagne tibétaine.»* (milieu) *«Jusqu'à présent, pour avoir accès à autant d'informations universelles, il aurait fallu que ton père soit un type drôlement influent.»* (en bas) *«Jusqu'à présent, pour avoir accès à autant d'informations universelles, il t'aurait fallu être entouré de gros gorilles et être le seul habilité à appuyer sur le fameux bouton.»*

PAGE 25 IMAGES 20-23 STUDENT *Dave Wasserman* SCHOOL *University of Delaware* PROGRAM *BFA, 1996* PROFESSORS *Raymond Nichols, Martha Carothers* ■ *These ads for the Internet use visual humor and playful Internet addresses to emphasize the diversity of subject matters one can explore on the Internet.* ● *Bei diesen Anzeigen mit humorvollen Bildern geht es um die Vielseitigkeit der via Internet zu erforschenden Themen.* ▲ *Annonces humoristiques mettant en avant la richesse des thèmes accessibles sur Internet.*

PAGE 26 IMAGES 24-26 STUDENTS *Ricki Dashkin, Jason Wright* SCHOOL *Portfolio Center* PROGRAM *Art Direction + Copywriting, 1996* PROFESSOR *Grady Phelan* ■ *"Cut the cord."* *This series promotes a radio-controlled mouse. Visuals suggest the freedom a cordless mouse can provide by emphasizing the constraints that cords maintain.* ● *«Schneide das Kabel durch.»* *Hier geht es um Werbung für kabellose Computermäuse, wobei die durch Kabel bedingten Einschränkungen demonstriert werden.* ▲ *«Coupe le câble!»* *Publicité pour des souris sans fil, montrant les inconvénients d'une souris «câblée».*

PAGE 27 IMAGES 27-29 STUDENTS *Chris Sailing, Karen Schwartz* SCHOOL *Portfolio Center* PROGRAM *Art Direction + Copywriting, 1996* PROFESSOR *Grady Phelan* ■ *This series promotes the financial services of investment specialists.* (top) *"In the past, an explorer's success was based on his fluency in maps and weather charts. Today, you don't even need to understand the stock pages."* (middle) *"While searching for their fortunes, explorers faced scurvy, mutiny and cannibals. Today you don't even have to leave the house."* (bottom) *"Once it took a queen's permission to launch a financial expedition, now it just takes a phone call."* ● *Werbung für die Dienstleistungen von Investmentspezialisten.* (Oben) *Früher hing der Erfolg eines Entdeckers von seiner Fähigkeit ab, Land- und Wetterkarten zu lesen. Heute muss man nicht mal die Börsenberichte verstehen.»* (Mitte) *«Auf der Suche nach ihrem Glück waren die Seefahrer früher Skorbut, Meuterei und Kannibalen ausgesetzt. Heute muss man dafür nicht einmal das Haus verlassen.»* (Unten) *«Früher bedurfte es der Erlaubnis einer Königin für eine Expedition, die die Finanzen aufbessern würde, heute bedarf es nur eines Anrufes.»* ▲ *Série d'annonces pour les services proposés par des professionnels en placements.* (en haut) *«Autrefois, le succès d'un explorateur dépendait de son talent à lire les cartes. Aujourd'hui, il n'est même pas nécessaire de comprendre les rapports boursiers.»* (milieu) *«Les marins en quête de trésors devaient affronter le scorbut, les mutineries et les cannibales. Aujourd'hui, il n'est même pas nécessaire de sortir de chez soi.»* (en bas) *«Il fut un temps où il fallait la bénédiction de la reine pour se lancer dans une expédition destinée à renflouer le Trésor. Aujourd'hui, un simple coup de fil suffit.»*

PAGE 28 IMAGES 30 STUDENT *Shawn Brown* SCHOOL *Portfolio Center* PROGRAM *Art Direction, 1996* PROFESSOR *Grady Phelan* ■ *"Human Jeans. It's in your blood. It's in our jeans."* ● *«Human Jeans. Du hast es im Blut. Es ist in unseren Jeans.»* ▲ *«Human Jeans. Tu les as dans le sang. C'est dans nos jeans.»*

PAGE 28 IMAGE 31 STUDENTS *Norris Post, Shannon Easter* SCHOOL *Portfolio Center* PROGRAM *Art Direction, 1996* PROFESSOR *Grady Phelan* ■ *"We're looking at things differently. Namely you. Personal pair."* *This ad promotes Levi's and a personal fit.* ● *«Wir betrachten die Dinge anders. Ganz besonders Dich. Ein persönliches Paar (Jeans).»* *Werbung für Levi's Jeans mit individuellem Schnitt.* ▲ *«Nous voyons les choses différemment. Toi en particulier. Ta paire, rien qu'à toi.»* *Publicité Levi's pour des jeans épousant toutes les formes.*

PAGE 29 IMAGES 32-34 STUDENT *Sharon Tao* SCHOOL *Portfolio Center* PROGRAM *Copywriting, 1996* PROFESSOR *Ed Chambliss*

PAGE 30 IMAGES 35-37 STUDENT *Cheryl Bernett* SCHOOL *University of Delaware* PROGRAM *BFA, 1996* PROFESSORS *Raymond Nichols, Martha Carothers*

PAGE 31 IMAGE 38 STUDENT *Jules Tan* SCHOOL *Swinburne University of Technology* PROGRAM *BA Graphic Design, 3rd year* ■ *Advertisement for a dessert bar.* ● *Anzeige für eine Dessert-Bar.* ▲ *Publicité pour un bar à desserts.*

PAGE 31 IMAGE 39 STUDENT *Ned Brown Sterns* SCHOOL *Portfolio Center* PROGRAM *Copywriting, 1996* PROFESSOR *Ed Chambliss*

PAGE 32 IMAGES 40-41 STUDENT *Kevin Stoohs* SCHOOL *School of Visual Arts* PROGRAM *BFA, 1996* PROFESSOR *Jeffrey Metzner* ■ *Ad for Starbucks coffee.* ● *Anzeigen für Starbucks-Kaffee.* ▲ *Publicités pour les cafés Starbucks.*

PAGE 32 IMAGES 42-43 STUDENT *Keri Roy* SCHOOL *School of Visual Arts* PROGRAM *BFA, 1996* PROFESSOR *Jeffrey Metzner* ■ *Ad for Starbucks coffee.* ● *Anzeigen für Starbucks-Kaffee.* ▲ *Publicités pour les cafés Starbucks.*

PAGE 32 IMAGE 44 STUDENT *Lauren Barrocas* SCHOOL *School of Visual Arts* PROGRAM *BFA, 1996* PROFESSOR *Jeffrey Metzner* CLASS *Alternative Portfolio*

PAGE 32 IMAGE 45 STUDENT *Tim Schultheis* SCHOOL *School of Visual Arts* PROGRAM *Special student status, Senior* PROFESSOR *Jeffrey Metzner* CLASS *Alternative Portfolio.* ■ *Ad for Starbucks coffee* ● *Anzeige für Starbucks-Kaffee.* ▲ *Publicités pour les cafés Starbucks.*

PAGE 33 IMAGE 46 STUDENT *Bradford Emmett* SCHOOL *School of Visual Arts* PROGRAM *BFA, 1996*

PAGE 33 IMAGES 47-49 STUDENTS *Tracy Bull, Mercy Burwell, Lois Eiler* SCHOOL *Portfolio Center* PROGRAM *Art Direction + Copywriting, 1996* PROFESSOR *Grady Phelan*

PAGE 34 IMAGE 50 STUDENT *Aki Inoue* SCHOOL *School of Visual Arts* PROGRAM *BFA, 1996* PROFESSOR *Jeffrey Metzner* ■ *Print campaign for Tower Records.* ● *Anzeigen-Kampagne für Tower Records.* ▲ *Campagne publicitaire pour Tower Records.*

PAGE 35 IMAGE 51 STUDENT *Christopher H. Yates* SCHOOL *School of Visual Arts* PROGRAM *BFA, Advertising, 1996* PROFESSOR *Jeffrey Metzner* CLASS *Alternative Portfolio* ■ *Two-page spread for Tower Records.* ● *Doppelseitige Anzeige für Tower Records.* ▲ *Annonce double page pour Tower Records.*

PAGE 35 IMAGE 52 STUDENT *Keri Roy* SCHOOL *School of Visual Arts* PROGRAM *BFA, 1996* PROFESSOR *Jeffrey Metzner* ■ *Print campaign for Tower Records.* ● *Anzeigenkampagne für Tower Records.* ▲ *Campagne publicitaire pour Tower Records.*

PAGE 36 IMAGES 53-55 STUDENT *Lenny Monfredo* SCHOOL *School of Visual Arts* PROGRAM *BFA* PROFESSOR *Jeffrey Metzner* ■ *Print campaign for Tower Records. "Whatever the message, we have the music."* ● *Anzeigen-Kampagne für Tower Records: «Was auch immer die Botschaft, wir haben die Musik.»* ▲ *Campagne publicitaire pour Tower Records. «Peu importe le ton, nous avons la musique.»*

PAGE 37 IMAGES 56, 57 STUDENT *Keri Roy* SCHOOL *School of Visual Arts* PROGRAM *BFA, 1996* PROFESSOR *Jeffrey Metzner* ■ *Print campaign for Tower Records.* ● *Anzeigenkampagne für Tower Records.* ▲ *Campagne publicitaire pour Tower Records.*

PAGE 38 IMAGES 58-61 STUDENTS *Jenni Kelly, Karen Schwartz* SCHOOL *Portfolio Center* PROGRAM *Art Direction + Copywriting, 1996* PROFESSOR *Grady Phelan* ■ *(top) "It's not supposed to hurt." (bottom, left) "Dry sex causes uncomfortable friction for you and your partner." (bottom right) "Prolonged dry sex is the leading cause of popped condoms."* ● *(Oben) «Es sollte nicht wehtun.» (Unten links) «Eine trockene Scheide ist für Sie und Ihren Partner unangenehm.» (Unten rechts) «Längerer Sex bei trockener Scheide ist die häufigste Ursache für geplatzte Kondome.»* ▲ *(en haut) «Cela ne devrait pas faire mal.» (en bas à gauche) «La sécheresse du vagin peut être source d'inconfort pour vous et votre partenaire.» (en bas à droite) «La sécheresse du vagin lors de rapports sexuels prolongés est la principale cause pouvant entraîner la déchirure d'un préservatif.»*

PAGE 39 IMAGES 62, 63 STUDENT *Karen Gergely* SCHOOL *University of Delaware* PROGRAM *Bachelor of Fine Art, 1996* PROFESSORS *Raymond Nichols, Martha Carothers* ■ *(top) "Wisdom is collected experience. And we've been collecting since 1884."* ● *(Oben) «Weisheit bedeutet gesammelte Erfahrungen. Wir sammeln seit 1884.»* ▲ *(en haut) «La sagesse est la somme des expériences. Nous en faisons depuis 1884.»*

PAGE 40 IMAGE 64 STUDENT *Christian Baffa* SCHOOL *School of Visual Arts* PROGRAM *BFA, 1996* ■ *"Monday, S.A.T.'s. Tuesday, love letter to girlfriend. 3rd period, math quiz. Wednesday, lunch table. Friday, girlfriend needs her space. S.A.T. scores come back." Tagline: "The world's number one, number two pencil."* ● *«Montag Aufnahmeprüfung. Dienstag Liebesbrief an Freundin. Mathearbeit. Mittwoch Tisch fürs Mittagessen bestellen. Freitag Freundin braucht ihren Freiraum. Prüfung. Wir bekommen die Prüfungsergebnisse.» Die Moral von der Geschichte réserver une table au resto pour le déjeuner. Vendredi ma nana veut que je lui lâche les baskets. Résultats du test d'admission.» La morale de l'histoire Le crayon n° 2, le n° 1 mondial*

PAGE 40 IMAGE 65 STUDENT *Todd Brunner* SCHOOL *School of Visual Arts* PROGRAM *BFA, 1996* ■ *"This winter you could break more than just your shovel. A shovel only works as hard as you [do]."* ● *«In diesem Winter könntest Du Dir mehr brechen als nur die Schneeschaufel. Eine Schaufel arbeitet nur so hart wie Du selbst.»* ▲ *Cet hiver, tu pourras éviter de prendre une pelle sans avoir à retrousser tes manches!*

PAGE 41 IMAGES 66 STUDENT *Craig Ghiglione* SCHOOL *Portfolio Center* PROGRAM *Art Direction, 1996* PROFESSOR *Grady Phelan*

PAGE 42 IMAGES 67-72 STUDENT *Ulrich Broeske* SCHOOL *Fachhochschule Dortmund* PROGRAM *13th term, Graphic Design* PROFESSOR *K. Hesse* ■ *Campaign for a secondhand store.* ● *Kampagne für einen Gebrauchtwarenladen.* ▲ *Campagne pour une friperie.*

PAGE 43 IMAGE 73 STUDENT *Christian Baffa* SCHOOL *School of Visual Arts* PROGRAM *BFA, 1996*

PAGE 43 IMAGE 74 STUDENTS *Michael Zulawinski, Thomas Hurd, Brad Kaye* SCHOOL *Portfolio Center* PROGRAM *Art Direction + Copywriting, 1996* PROFESSOR *Grady Phelan*

PAGE 44 IMAGES 75, 76 STUDENT *Tim Schultheis* SCHOOL *School of Visual Arts* PROGRAM *Special student status, Senior* PROFESSOR *Jeffrey Metzner* CLASS *Alternative Portfolio* ■ *3m spray adhesive. "When you really need it to stick."* ● *3M-Spray-Kleber: «Wenn es wirklich halten muss.»* ▲ *Adhésif 3M en bombe. «Quand il faut vraiment que ça colle!»*

PAGE 44 IMAGE 77 STUDENT *Heather Plansker* SCHOOL *School of Visual Arts* PROGRAM *BFA, 1996* ■ *"It takes some strong tape to shut him up."* ● *«Man braucht ein starkes Klebband, damit er den Mund hält.»* ▲ *«Pour lui clouer le caquet, il faut un ruban super adhésif.»*

PAGE 44 IMAGE 78 STUDENT *Tim Schultheis* SCHOOL *School of Visual Arts* PROGRAM *Special student status, Senior* PROFESSOR *Jeffrey Metzner* CLASS *Alternative Portfolio* ■ *3m spray adhesive. "When you really need it to stick."* ● *3M-Spray-Kleber «Wenn es wirklich halten muss.»* ▲ *Adhésif 3M en bombe. «Quand il faut vraiment que ça colle!»*

PAGE 44 IMAGE 79 STUDENT *Frank Martino* SCHOOL *School of Visual Arts* PROGRAM *BFA, 1996* ■ *"Unlikely bonds."* ● *«Unwahrscheinliche Bindungen.»* ▲ *«Liaisons improbables.»*

PAGE 44 IMAGE 80 STUDENT *Lenny Monfredo* SCHOOL *School of Visual Arts* PROGRAM *BFA, 1996* PROFESSORS *Jack Mariucci, Jeffrey Metzner*

PAGE 44 IMAGE 81 STUDENT *Todd Brunner* SCHOOL *School of Visual Arts* PROGRAM *BFA, 1996* PROFESSOR *Jeffrey Metzner* ■ *3m spray adhesive.* ● *3M-Spraykleber.* ▲ *Adhésif 3M en bombe.*

PAGE 44 IMAGE 82 STUDENT *Lenny Monfredo* SCHOOL *School of Visual Arts* PROGRAM *BFA* PROFESSOR *Jeffrey Metzner* ■ *3m spray adhesive.* ● *3M-Spraykleber.* ▲ *Adhésif 3M en bombe.*

PAGE 45 IMAGE 83 STUDENT *Marco Morsella* SCHOOL *School of Visual Arts* PROGRAM *BFA, 1996* ■ *"If it makes a difference, we also sell clear tape."* ● *«Wenn es darauf ankommt, verkaufen wir auch transparentes Klebband.»* ▲ *«S'il le faut, nous vendons aussi des rubans adhésifs transparents.»*

PAGE 45 IMAGE 84 STUDENT *Lauren Barrocas* SCHOOL *School of Visual Arts* PROGRAM *BFA, 1996* PROFESSOR *Jeffrey Metzner* ■ *3m spray adhesive.* ● *Werbung für 3M-Spraykleber.* ▲ *Publicité pour l'adhésif 3M en bombe.*

PAGE 46 IMAGE 85 STUDENT *Bradford Emmett* SCHOOL *School of Visual Arts* PROGRAM *BFA, 1996* ■ *"If you think nobody reads the ENQUIRER, explain why we've been sued over 15,000 times. The whole truth, and nothing but the truth, kinda."* ● *«Wenn Sie glauben, dass niemand THE ENQUIRER liest, erklären Sie uns, warum wir 15000 mal verklagt worden sind. Die ganze Wahrheit und nichts als die Wahrheit, ...so ziemlich.»* ▲ *«Si vous croyez que personne ne lit THE ENQUIRER, expliquez-nous pourquoi on nous a intenté 15 000 procès. La vérité, toute la vérité, ...ou presque!»*

PAGE 46 IMAGE 86 STUDENT *Lenny Monfredo* SCHOOL *School of Visual Arts* PROGRAM *BFA, 1996*

PAGE 47 IMAGES 87-89 STUDENTS *Andreas Pawlitzki, Carsten Bolk* SCHOOL *Universität Gesamthochschule Essen* PROGRAM *Communications Design, 10th semester* ■ *"Not all trash gets recycled. Some gets printed."* ● *«Nicht jeder Abfall wird wiederverwertet. Mancher wird auch gedruckt.»* ▲ *«Tous les déchets ne sont pas recyclés. Certains sont imprimés.»*

PAGE 48 IMAGE 90 STUDENT *Dana Betgilan* SCHOOL *School of Visual Arts* PROGRAM *BFA, 1996* ■ *Print campaign for German newspapers. Above: "A Y. Read, think, contribute." (Center) "A nail. " (Below) "A pear." The idea behind this campaign is that things are sometimes not what they seem.* ● *Bei dieser Aktion der Zeitungen in Deutschland geht es darum, dass die Dinge oft anders sind, als sie scheinen bzw. anders dargestellt werden, als sie sind.* ▲ *Campagne presse pour les quotidiens allemands. (en haut) «Un 'Y' Lisez, pensez, participez! » (au milieu) «Un clou.» (en bas) «Une poire.» Il s'agissait de montrer que les apparences sont souvent trompeuses.*

PAGE 48 IMAGE 91 STUDENT *Mei Yap* SCHOOL *School of Visual Arts* PROGRAM *BFA, 1996* ■ *"The next time you throw food in the trash, think twice. There's a better way to feed the homeless."* ● *«Wenn Du nächstes Mal Lebensmittel wegwirfst, denk nach. Es gibt einen besseren Weg, den Obdachlosen zu essen zu geben.»* ▲ *«La prochaine fois que tu jetteras de la nourriture, penses-y! Il existe d'autres moyens de venir en aide aux sans-abri!»*

PAGE 48 IMAGES 92, 93 STUDENT *Keri Roy* SCHOOL *School of Visual Arts* PROGRAM *BFA, 1996* PROFESSOR *Jeffrey Metzner* ■ *Advertisement for a ficticious group, The Coalition of Smokers for a Smoking America.* ● *Werbung für eine fiktive Gruppe, die «Vereinigung der Raucher für ein rauchendes Amerika».* ▲ *Publicité pour un groupe fictif, l'association des fumeurs pour une Amérique... fumante!*

PAGE 49 IMAGE 94 STUDENT *Craig Ghiglione* SCHOOL *Portfolio Center* PROGRAM *Art Direction, 1996* PROFESSOR *Grady Phelan*

PAGE 50 IMAGE 95 STUDENT *Sarah Clackson* SCHOOL *Somerset College of Arts & Technology, School of Communication and Performing Arts* PROFESSOR *Jack Gardner* ■ *Campaign for a voluntary euthanasia society.* ● *Kampagne zugunsten der Sterbehilfe auf Verlangen.* ▲ *Campagne pour le droit à l'euthanasie.*

PAGE 50 IMAGE 96 STUDENT *James Foss* SCHOOL *Somerset College of Arts & Technology, School of Communication and Performing Arts* PROFESSOR *Jack Gardner* ■ *"To save a man against his will is the same as killing him."* ● *«Einen Menschen gegen seinen Willen zu retten bedeutet soviel, wie ihn zu töten.»* ▲ *«Sauver un être humain contre son gré, c'est comme le tuer.»*

PAGE 50 IMAGES 97, 98 STUDENT *Rebecca Edwards* SCHOOL *Somerset College of Arts & Technology, School of Communication and Performing Arts* PROFESSOR *Jack Gardner* ■ *Campaign for London Friend, counseling helplines and support for lesbians and gay men.* ● *Kampagne für London Friend, ein Telephonberatungsdienst für Lesbierinnen und Homosexuelle.* ▲ *Campagne pour London Friend, un service téléphonique s'adressant aux lesbiennes et aux homosexuels.*

PAGE 51 IMAGES 99-104 STUDENT *Jan Koemmet* SCHOOL *Bergische Universität Wuppertal* PROGRAM *10th semester, Communication Design* PROFESSOR *Uwe Loesch* ■ *"Masking of identity," a campaign for the Green Party in Germany.* ● *Kampagne für die Grünen in Deutschland.* ▲ *Campagne du parti des Verts en Allemagne.*

PAGE 52 IMAGES 105, 106 STUDENT *Lauren S. Barrocas* SCHOOL *School of Visual Arts* PROGRAM *BFA, 1996* PROFESSOR *Jeffrey Metzner* ■ *"Our jackets have a lifetime guarantee. You don't."* ● *«Unsere Jacken haben eine lebenslange Garantie. Sie nicht.»* ▲ *«Nos vestes sont garanties à vie. Vous non.»*

PAGE 53 IMAGE 107 STUDENT *Mark Townsley* SCHOOL *School of Visual Arts* PROGRAM *BFA, 1996* PROFESSOR *Jeffrey Metzner* ■ *Advertisement for Northface.* ● *Anzeige für Sport- und Freizeitkleidung von Northface.* ▲ *Publicité Northface.*

PAGE 53 IMAGE 108 STUDENT *Tim Schultheis* SCHOOL *School of Visual Arts* CLASS *Alternative Portfolio* PROFESSOR *Jeffrey Metzner* ■ *Advertisement for Northface.* ● *Anzeige für Sport- und Freizeitkleidung von Northface.* ▲ *Publicité Northface.*

PAGE 54 IMAGES 109, 110 STUDENT *Cherser Kow* SCHOOL *School of Visual Arts* PROGRAM *BFA Graphic Design, 1996* PROFESSOR *Jeffrey Keyton* CLASS *Senior Portfolio* ■ *(top left) "You need some clothes?"* ● *Oben link: «Sie brauchen etwas zum Anziehen?»* ▲ *(en haut à gauche) «Il vous faut des vêtements?»*

PAGE 54 IMAGES 111, 112 STUDENT *Jin Oh* SCHOOL *School of Visual Arts* PROGRAM *BFA, 1996* PROFESSOR *Jeffrey Metzner* CLASS *Alternative Portfolio* ■ *Advertisements for Nike featuring Dennis Rodman.* ● *Anzeigen für Nike mit Basketball-Spieler Dennis Rodman.* ▲ *Annonce Nike avec Dennis Rodman.*

PAGE 55 IMAGE 113 STUDENT *Bradford Emmett* SCHOOL *School of Visual Arts* PROGRAM *BFA, 1996* ■ *Advertisement for Bell Helmets. "Because motorcycles don't have airbags."* ● *Werbung für Motorradhelme «Weil Motorräder keine Airbags haben.»* ▲ *Publicité pour des casques de moto: «Parce que votre deux-roues n'a pas d'airbag.»*

PAGE 56 IMAGE 114 STUDENT *Keri Roy* SCHOOL *School of Visual Arts* PROGRAM *BFA, 1996* PROFESSOR *Jeffrey Metzner* ■ *The assignment was to name a skateboard company and develop an ad.* ● *Anzeige für eine Skateboard-Firma.* ▲ *L'objectif était de créer une annonce pour un fabricant de skate-boards et d'intégrer le nom de la marque.*

PAGE 56 IMAGE 115 STUDENT *Lenny Monfredo* SCHOOL *School of Visual Arts* PROGRAM *BFA* PROFESSOR *Jeffrey Metzner* ■ *The assignment was to name a skateboard company and develop an ad.* ● *Hier ging es um eine Kampagne für einen Skateboard-Hersteller.* ▲ *L'objectif assigné était de créer une annonce pour un fabricant de skate-boards et d'intégrer le nom de la marque.*

PAGE 56 IMAGE 116 STUDENT *Mark Townsley* SCHOOL *School of Visual Arts* PROGRAM *BFA, 1996* PROFESSOR *Jeffrey Metzner* ■ *Advertisement for a fictional skateboard company.* ● *Werbung für einen fiktiven Skateboard-Hersteller.* ▲ *Publicité pour un fabricant fictif de skate-boards.*

PAGE 57 IMAGE 117 STUDENT *Kevin Stoohs* SCHOOL *School of Visual Arts* PROGRAM *BFA, 1996* PROFESSOR *Jeffrey Metzner* ■ *Advertisement for a fictional skateboard company.* ● *Werbung für einen fiktiven Skateboard-Hersteller.* ▲ *Publicité pour un fabricant fictif de skate-boards.*

PAGE 57 IMAGE 118 STUDENT *Tim Schultheis* SCHOOL *School of Visual Arts* PROGRAM *Special student status, Senior* PROFESSOR *Jeffrey Metzner* CLASS *Alternative Portfolio* ■ *Advertisement for a fictional skateboard company.* ● *Werbung für einen fiktiven Skateboard-Hersteller.* ▲ *Publicité pour un fabricant fictif de skate-boards.*

PAGE 58, 59 IMAGES 119-130 STUDENT *Lutz Widmaier* SCHOOL *Staatliche Akademie der Bildenden Künste* PROGRAM *10th semester, Graphic Design* PROFESSOR *Heinz Edelmann* ■ *Poster campaign for the Frankfurt zoo.* ● *Werbeplakate für den Frankfurter Zoo.* ▲ *Campagne pour le zoo de Francfort.*

PAGE 60 IMAGES 131, 132 STUDENT *Sibila del Mar Munoz* SCHOOL *School of Visual Arts* PROGRAM *BFA, 1996* ■ *(left) "Come do some lines with us." (right) "You've seen it in* VOGUE. *Now see it live."* ● *Zoo-Werbung. Links: Wortspiel. "To do some lines" ist Slang für das Schnupfen von Kokain, hier auf die Streifen des Zebras bezogen. Rechts «Sie haben es in* VOGUE *gesehen. Sehen Sie es jetzt in der Realität.»* ▲ *(à gauche) «Sacré coco!» (à droite) «Vous l'avez vu dans* VOGUE. *Maintenant, voyez-le de vos propres yeux!»*

PAGE 61 IMAGES 133, 134 STUDENT *Tom Dowd* SCHOOL *School of Visual Arts* PROGRAM *BFA, 1996* PROFESSOR *Jack Mariucci*

PAGE 62 IMAGE 135 STUDENT *Aki Inoue* SCHOOL *School of Visual Arts* PROGRAM *BFA, 1996*

PAGE 63 IMAGES 136-143 STUDENT *Thimoteus Ibykus Wagner* SCHOOL *Universität Gesamthochschule Essen* PROGRAM *Communications Design, 10th semester* PROFESSORS *Otto Näscher, Vilim Vasata* ■ *International tourism campaign for Germany.* ● *Internationale Kampagne zur Förderung des Tourismus in Deutschland.* ▲ *Campagne internationale visant à promouvoir le tourisme en Allemagne.*

PAGE 64 IMAGES 144-146 STUDENT *Jeff Dey* SCHOOL *University of North Texas* PROGRAM *Communication Design, Senior* PROFESSOR *Eric Ligon* CLASS *Publication Design* ■ *(top) "Rethink" (bottom) "A reworking of what we design, how we design it and where we are going." This annual report for Herman Miller compares external structure of furniture to internal corporate structure and serves as a handbook for restructuring the company.* ● *(Oben) «Überdenken.» (Unten) «Eine Überarbeitung dessen, was wir entwerfen und wie wir es entwerfen und eine Richtungsänderung.» Der Jahresbericht für den Möbelfabrikanten Herman Miller vergleicht äussere Strukturen von Möbeln mit internen Firmenstrukturen und dient als Handbuch für die Umstrukturierung der Firma.* ▲ *(en haut) «A repenser.» (en bas) «Nous avons retravaillé ce que nous avions créé, revu le concept et reconsidéré l'objectif poursuivi.» Le rapport annuel d'Herman Miller compare la «superstructure» de meubles avec la structure interne d'une entreprise et tient lieu de manuel pour restructurer une société.*

PAGE 65 IMAGES 147-154 STUDENT *Katja Kleinebrecht* SCHOOL *Fachhochschule Dortmund* PROGRAM *Graphic Design, 11th semester* PROFESSOR *Dieter Ziegenfeuter* ■ *A book whose theme is the color red.* ● *Diplomarbeit: Ein sinnliches Buch über die Farbe Rot.* ▲ *Travail de diplôme. Livre sensuel sur la couleur rouge.*

PAGE 66, 67 IMAGES 155-170 STUDENTS *Lutz Eberle, Andreas Jung, Marcus Wichmann, Hans Pfrommer* SCHOOL *Staatliche Akademie der Bildenden Künste* PROGRAM *Graphic Design, 11th semester* PROFESSOR *Manfred Kröplien* ■ *Digital project and a playful exploration of typography. On disk in the back of the book, the reader finds a custom designed font with which some of the book is printed. The font is encrypted and the password can be obtained by solving a crossword puzzle embedded in the text.* ● *«Lahm Ausgabe Nr. 4» ist ein rein digitales Projekt, bei dem es um spielerischen Umgang mit*

Typographie ging. Hinten im Buch befindet sich eine Diskette, die dem Leser eine speziell für das Buch entworfene Schrift liefert. Das Passwort dafür erhält man, wenn man ein kleines, im Text enthaltenes Kreuzworträtsel löst. ▲ Projet numérique pour une incursion ludique dans le monde de la typographie. Une disquette, livrée avec l'ouvrage, fournit une police d'écriture spécialement créée pour celui-ci. Pour ouvrir la disquette, il faut d'abord trouver le mot de passe en résolvant un mots croisés figurant dans le livre.

PAGE 68 IMAGES 171-173 STUDENT *Deklah Polansky* SCHOOL *School of Visual Arts* PROGRAM *BFA, 1996* PROFESSOR *Stacy Dramond* ■ *Book for the work of the Starn Twins.* ● *Buch über die Arbeit der Starn-Zwillinge, Photographen, deren grossformatige Aufnahmen und Montage sehr malerisch wirken.* ▲ *Livre consacré au travail des frères jumeaux Starn.*

PAGE 69 IMAGE 174 STUDENT *Sha-Mayne Chan* SCHOOL *School of Visual Arts* PROGRAM *Graphic Design, 1996* PROFESSOR *Carin Goldberg* ■ *Series book cover design on books by John Berger.* ● *Umschlaggestaltung für eine Buchserie.* ▲ *Réalisation de couvertures pour une série de livres.*

PAGE 69 IMAGE 175 STUDENTS *Lutz Eberle, Andreas Jung, Hans Pfrommer, Marcus Wichmann* SCHOOL *Staatliche Akademie der Bildenden Künste* PROGRAM *Graphic Design, 11th semester* PROFESSOR *Manfred Kröplien* ■ *The pages in this book are silver-coated. The reader can use the 1 mark coin provided on the cover to rub off the coating and allow four "dream cars" to appear.* ● *Mit der Mark auf dem Umschlag kann der Leser die Silberbeschichtung der Buchseiten wegrubbeln, woraufhin vier «Traumautos» zum Vorschein kommen.* ▲ *Le lecteur peut gratter les pages du livre à l'aide du mark se trouvant sur la couverture et découvrir ainsi quatre «voitures de rêve».*

PAGE 69 IMAGE 176 STUDENT *So Takahashi* SCHOOL *School of Visual Arts* PROGRAM *BFA, 1996* PROFESSOR *Chris Austopchuck* CLASS *Portfolio* ■ *Albert Camus book cover design.* ● *Umschlag für ein Buch von Albert Camus.* ▲ *Couverture pour un livre d'Albert Camus.*

PAGE 70 IMAGES 177-184 STUDENT *Charlotte Löbner* SCHOOL *Fachhochschule Mainz* PROGRAM *Design* PROFESSOR *Ulrike Stoltz* ■ *Book on the subject of hair: "Along the hair line."* ● *Auseinandersetzung mit dem Thema «Haare»* ▲ *Livre consacré aux cheveux.*

PAGE 71 IMAGES 185-192 STUDENT *Elke Götz* SCHOOL *Staatliche Akademie der Bildenden Künste* PROGRAM *Graphic Design, 8th semester* PROFESSOR *Hans-Georg Pospischil* ■ *Illustration and design of a short story by Italo Calvino.* ● *Illustration und Gestaltung der Kurzgeschichte «Die Entfernung des Mondes» aus dem Band «Das Gedächtnis der Welten» von Italo Calvino.* ▲ *Illustration et conception graphique d'une nouvelle d'Italo Calvino.*

PAGE 72 IMAGES 193-199 STUDENT *Machiko Matsufuji* SCHOOL *School of Visual Arts* PROGRAM *BFA, Graphic Design 1996* PROFESSOR *Christopher Austopchuck*

PAGE 73 IMAGE 200 STUDENT *Hubie Le* SCHOOL *Portfolio Center* PROGRAM *Graphic Design, 1996* PROFESSOR *Hank Richardson*

PAGE 73 IMAGES 201-202 STUDENT *Marcus Wichmann* SCHOOL *Staatliche Akademie der Bildenden Künste* PROGRAM *Graphic Design* PROFESSOR *Manfred Kröplien* ■ *"A file containing reality."* ● *Ein «Wirklichkeitssammelordner».* ▲ *Les dossiers de la réalité.*

PAGE 74 IMAGES 203-206 STUDENT *Andrew Reed* SCHOOL *Oregon State University* PROGRAM *BFA, 1996* PROFESSOR *David Hardesty*

PAGE 74 IMAGES 207-210 STUDENT *Amie Walter* SCHOOL *Oregon State University* PROGRAM *BFA, 1996* PROFESSOR *David Hardesty*

PAGE 75 IMAGE 211 STUDENT *Connie M. Hwang* SCHOOL *University of Washington* PROGRAM *MFA* PROFESSOR *Doug Wadden* ■ *Invitation to Dale Chihuly's college honor event.* ● *Einladung zu einer College-Feier.* ▲ *Invitation à la fête des étudiants.*

PAGE 76 IMAGES 212-218 STUDENT *Andria Davis, Abigail Fein* SCHOOL *University of Delaware* PROGRAM *Bachelor of Science, 1996* PROFESSORS *Martha Carothers, Raymond Nichols* ■ *Catalog for Saltwater Sole summer shoe selection.* ● *Katalog für den Schuhhersteller Saltwater Sole mit der neuen Sommerkollektion.* ▲ *Catalogue Saltwater Sole présentant la nouvelle collection de chaussures pour l'été.*

PAGE 77 IMAGES 219-222 STUDENT *Abigail Fein* SCHOOL *University of Delaware* PROGRAM *Bachelor of Science, 1996* PROFESSORS *Martha Carothers, Ray Nichols* CLASS *Portfolio Preparation* ■ *"A Summer Day"- a visual and written interpretation of summer.* ● *«Ein Sommertag» – Eine Interpretation des Sommers in Text und Bild.* ▲ *«Une journée d'été» – interprétation de l'été en texte et en images.*

PAGE 77 IMAGE 223 STUDENT *Gabriel Kuo* SCHOOL *School of Visual Arts* PROGRAM *Graphic Design, 1996* PROFESSOR *Cris Gianakos* ■ *Cover for a museum catalog.* ● *Umschlag für einen Katalog des Design-Museums.* ▲ *Couverture réalisée pour le catalogue d'un musée du design.*

PAGE 77 IMAGES 224, 225 STUDENT *Ingrid Forbord* SCHOOL *School of Visual Arts* PROGRAM *BFA, 1996* PROFESSOR *Carin Goldberg* CLASS *Senior Portfolio* ■ *Spreads featuring Alvin Ailey and Aretha Franklin for a promotional booklet for PBS's "American Masters" series.* ● *Seiten mit Alvin Ailey und Aretha Franklin aus einer Werbebroschüre für die "American Masters" -Reihe des öffentlichen TV-Senders PBS.* ▲ *Alvin Ailey et Aretha Franklin. Pages extraites d'une brochure publicitaire pour l'émission culturelle American Masters consacrée aux grandes figures de l'Amérique et diffusée sur une chaîne publique.*

PAGE 78 IMAGES 226, 227 STUDENT *Geoff Kaplan* SCHOOL *Cranbrook Academy of Art* PROGRAM *MFA, 1996* PROFESSOR *Katherine McCoy* ■ *Art academy catalog for prospective students.* ● *Informationskatalog für Studienbewerber.* ▲ *Brochure informative s'adressant aux étudiants potentiels.*

PAGE 79 IMAGE 228 STUDENT *Gaby Brink* SCHOOL *California College of Arts & Crafts* PROGRAM *Graphic Design 3* PROFESSOR *Melanie Doherty* DEPARTMENT CHAIR *Michael Vanderbyl* ■ *Project: Museum of Tolerance Tabloid.* ● *Das Projekt: Ein Museum der Toleranz* ▲ *Le projet: Un musée de la tolérance*

PAGE 80 IMAGE 229 STUDENT *Tim Rogers* SCHOOL *University of South Australia* PROGRAM *Graphic Design, 4th year* PROFESSOR *Lyndon Whaite* ■ *This image was created for the "Australian Paper" calendar. The theme is "Australian Dreaming."* ● *Maiblatt für einen Kalender mit dem Thema: «Australische Träume». Er wirbt für australisches Papier.* ▲ *Calendrier publicitaire pour du papier australien. Thème: «Le Rêve australien».*

PAGE 81 IMAGES 230, 231 STUDENT *Gilmar Wendt* SCHOOL *Fachhochschule Mainz* PROGRAM *Communication Design* PROFESSOR *Roland Siegrist* ■ *Group project to develop an identity for the city of Mainz.* ● *Corporate-Identity-Programm für die Stadt Mainz.* ▲ *Programme d'identité visuelle pour la ville de Mayence.*

PAGE 81 IMAGE 232 STUDENT *Regina Krutoy* SCHOOL *School of Visual Arts* PROGRAM *BFA, 1996* PROFESSOR *Henrietta Condak* CLASS *Graphic Design* ■ *Identity created for a Japanese restaurant.* ● *Erscheinungsbild für ein japanisches Restaurant.* ▲ *Identité visuelle créée pour un restaurant japonais.*

PAGE 81 IMAGE 233 STUDENT *Michael Tompert* SCHOOL *Academy of Art College* PROGRAM *BFA, 1996* ■ *Corporate identity project.* ● *C.I. Programm.* ▲ *Programme d'identité visuelle.*

PAGE 81 IMAGE 234 STUDENT *Kelly Holohan* SCHOOL *Tyler School of Art* PROGRAM *MFA, Visual Design, 1996* PROFESSOR *Alice E. Drueding* ■ *Bread bags and menu for Big Sky Bread Company.* ● *Brottüten und Speisekarte der Big Sky Bread-Cafés.* ▲ *Sachets et carte des cafés Big Sky Bread.*

PAGE 81 IMAGE 235 STUDENT *Angela Schroeder* SCHOOL *Fachhochschule Mainz* PROFESSOR *Olaf Leu* CLASS *Corporate Identity Design* ■ *Corporate identity for a music publisher.* ● *C.I. Programm.* ▲ *Programme d'identité visuelle.*

PAGES 82, 83 IMAGES 236-240 STUDENT *Katherine Szeto* SCHOOL *University Of Missouri at Columbia* PROGRAM *BA, Senior* ■ *Identity for a fictional AIA traveling exhibit that conveys the ideas, methodology, and work of Russian Constructivist architect Konstantin Melnikov.* ● *Graphisches Erscheinungsbild für eine Wanderausstellung, die ein fiktives amerikanisches Institut für Architektur den Ideen, der Methodik und den Arbeiten des Architekten Konstantin Melnikov widmet, einem Vertreter des russischen Konstruktivismus.* ▲ *Identité visuelle créée pour l'exposition itinérante d'un institut d'architectes fictif. L'exposition était consacrée aux idées, à la méthodologie et aux travaux de l'architecte Konstantin Melnikov, représentant du constructivisme russe.*

PAGE 84 IMAGES 241-245 STUDENT *Amanda Pounds* SCHOOL *University of North Texas* PROGRAM *BFA, 1996* PROFESSOR *Meta Newhouse* CLASS *Senior Portfolio* ■ *Campaign and comprehensive identity system for an upscale store and distributor of fine breads and cakes.* ● *Kampagne und umfangreiches C.I.-Programm für eine erstklassige Bäckerei, die Brote und Kuchen im eigenen Geschäft verkauft und auch andere beliefert.* ▲ *Campagne et vaste programme d'identité visuelle réalisés pour une boulangerie-pâtisserie réputée.*

PAGE 85 IMAGE 246 STUDENT *Tara Benyei* SCHOOL *Academy of Art College* PROGRAM *BFA, 1995-1996* PROFESSOR *Howard York* CLASS *Corporate Systems* ■ *Corporate identity for SPECTRUM.* ● *C.I. für SPECTRUM.* ▲ *Identité institutionnelle de SPECTRUM.*

PAGE 86 IMAGE 247 STUDENT *Steve Clifton* SCHOOL *Portfolio Center* PROGRAM *Graphic Design, 1996* PROFESSOR *Hank Richardson*

PAGE 87 IMAGE 248 STUDENT *Suzanne Ach* SCHOOL *School of Visual Arts* PROGRAM *BFA Graphic Design, 1996* PROFESSOR *Carin Goldberg* ■ *Covers for "Picture," a photography magazine.* ● *Umschläge für PICTURE, ein Photomagazin.* ▲ *Pages de couverture réalisées pour le magazine photo PICTURE.*

PAGE 88 IMAGES 249-254 STUDENT *Kerstin Hamburg* SCHOOL *Bergische Universität Wuppertal* PROGRAM *12th semester* PROFESSORS *Bazon Brock, Marc Itzikowiz, Uwe Loesch* ■ *Project title: "Masking of Identity"* ● *Redaktionelle Gestaltung.* ▲ *Projet rédactionnel intitulé «L'identité voilée.*

PAGE 89 IMAGES 255-262 STUDENT *Barbara Melluso* SCHOOL *School of Visual Arts* PROGRAM *BFA Graphic Design, 1996* PROFESSOR *Carin Goldberg*

PAGES 90, 91 IMAGES 263-271 STUDENT *Ingo Ditges* SCHOOL *Staatliche Akademie der Bildenden Künste* PROGRAM *6th Semester, Graphic Design* PROFESSOR *Hans-Georg Pospischil* ■ *Music magazine for teenagers.* ● *Musikzeitschrift für Teenies.* ▲ *Magazine pour ados consacré à la musique.*

PAGE 91 IMAGE 272 STUDENT *Karin Kaiser* SCHOOL *Staatliche Akademie der Bildenden Künste* PROGRAM *Graphic Design, Thesis work* PROFESSOR *Hans-Georg Pospischil* ■ *"The White Male System." Concept and design of a magazine, which is always dedicated to one special subject.* ● *Konzeption und Gestaltung einer monothematischen Zeitschrift. «Das White Male System.»* ▲ *«Le sytème du Mâle blanc». Conception et réalisation d'un magazine consacré à un seul thème.*

PAGE 92 IMAGES 273-277 STUDENT *Karin Kaiser* SCHOOL *Staatliche Akademie der Bildenden Künste* PROGRAM *Graphic Design, Thesis work* PROFESSOR *Hans-Georg Pospischil* ■ *Concept and design of a magazine which treats single subjects in each issue. (top and bottom) Images for an article in the issue on the subject "Woman"; (center) Covers for issues on different subjects.* ● *Konzeption und Gestaltung einer monothematischen Zeitschrift. Oben und unten Bilder zu einem Artikel aus dem Themenheft «Frau»; Mitte Umschläge für verschiedene Themenhefte.* ▲ *Conception et réalisation d'un magazine consacré à un seul thème. (en haut et en bas) photos d'un article extrait d'un numéro consacré à la femme; (au milieu) couvertures de différents numéros.*

PAGE 93 IMAGE 278 STUDENT *Lisa Critchfield* SCHOOL *University of Utah* PROGRAM *BFA, Graphic Design, 1996-1997* PROFESSOR *Mac Magleby* CLASS *Visual Communications* ■ *Assignment: create a magazine masthead, cover, contents and features spread.* ● *Gestaltung des Impressums, des Umschlags, der Inhaltsseite und einer Artikelseite.* ▲ *Sujet Réaliser l'impressum, la page de couverture, le sommaire et une page d'un magazine.*

PAGE 93 IMAGE 279 STUDENT *James Scola* SCHOOL *School of Visual Arts* PROGRAM *BFA, 1996* PROFESSOR *Chris Austopchak* ■ *Magazine entitled "Visual Activism" which deals with social, political and economic issues.* ● *Zeitschrift mit dem Titel Visual Activism, die sich mit sozialen, politischen und wirtschaftlichen Themen befasst.* ▲ *Magazine intitulé Visual Activism, traitant de problèmes sociaux, politiques et économiques.*

PAGE 93 IMAGE 280 STUDENT *Peter Lederle* SCHOOL *Staatliche Akademie der Bildenden Künste* PROGRAM *4th semester, Graphic Design* PROFESSOR *Günter Jacki* ■ *Cover for a trade magazine on applied electronics.* ● *Umschlag für eine Fachzeitschrift.* ▲ *Couverture pour un magazine spécialisé.*

PAGE 93 IMAGE 281 STUDENT *Börge B. Bredenberk* SCHOOL *Kent Institute of Art & Design* PROGRAM *BA, Communications, Media, Illustration, 6th term* ■ *Design of a new youth culture magazine with a circulation of 3000.* ● *Gestaltung eines neuen Jugend-Kulturmagazins mit einer Auflage von 3000 Stück.* ▲ *Conception d'un nouveau magazine culturel pour les jeunes, tiré à 3000 exemplaires.*

PAGE 94 IMAGES 282-287 STUDENT *Katja Dell* SCHOOL *Staatliche Akademie der Bildenden Künste* PROGRAM *Graphic Design, 5th semester* PROFESSOR *Hans-Georg Pospischil* ■ *Cover for a fictitious magazine entitled «& more.»* ● *Umschlag für ein fiktives Magazin mit dem Titel '& more'.* ▲ *Couverture d'un magazine fictif intitulé «& more.»*

PAGE 95 IMAGES 288, 289 STUDENT *Ingo Ditges* SCHOOL *Staatliche Akademie der Bildenden Künste* PROGRAM *Graphic Design, 6th semester* PROFESSOR *Hans-Georg Pospischil* ■ *Two spreads from a magazine on the subject of snowboarding.* ● *Doppelseiten aus einem Magazin zum Thema 'Snowboarden'.* ▲ *Doubles pages d'un magazine consacré au snowboard.*

PAGE 95 IMAGES 290, 291 STUDENT *Elif Memisoglu* SCHOOL *School of Visual Arts* PROGRAM *BFA, Graphic Design, 1996* PROFESSOR *Carin Goldberg* ■ *Editorial promotion for the "American Master" series on the Public Broadcasting System.* ● *Redaktionelle Promotion der amerikanischen «Meisterserie» eines öffentlichen TV-Senders.* ▲ *Publicité rédactionnelle pour une série consacrée aux grandes figures de l'Amérique, diffusée sur une chaîne publique.*

PAGE 95 IMAGES 292, 293 STUDENT *James Scola* SCHOOL *School of Visual Arts* PROGRAM *BFA, 1996* PROFESSOR *Chris Austopchuk* ■ *Magazine entitled "Visual Activism" which deals with social, political and economic issues.* ● *Gestaltung einer Zeitschrift mit dem Titel «Visual Activism,» die sich mit sozialen, politischen und ökonomischen Themen befasst.* ▲ *Magazine intitulé «Visual Activism,» traitant de problèmes sociaux, politiques et économiques.*

PAGE 95 IMAGES 294, 295 STUDENT *Tamara Behar* SCHOOL *School of Visual Arts* PROGRAM *Bachelor of Arts, 1996* PROFESSOR *Carin Goldberg* ■ *A spread on Robert Frank for a high-end photography magazine.* ● *Gestaltung einer anspruchsvollen Photozeitschrift, hier eine Seite, die über den Inhalt informiert und eine Doppelseite über den Photographen Robert Frank.* ▲ *Réalisation d'un magazine photo haut de gamme. Sommaire et double page sur le photographe Robert Frank.*

PAGE 96 IMAGES 296-299 STUDENT *Deborah Bowman* SCHOOL *California College of Arts & Crafts* CLASS *Graphic Design 5* PROFESSOR *Michael Vanderbyl* ■ *Thesis project "Breathing Life into the Fear of Inadequacy."* ● *Abschlussarbeit «Der Angst vor Unzulänglichkeit Leben einhauchen.»* ▲ *Travail de fin d'études intitulé «Insuffler la vie à la peur de l'insuffisance.»*

PAGE 97 IMAGES 300, 301 STUDENT *Shandele Gumucio* SCHOOL *California College of Arts & Crafts* CLASS *Graphic Design 3* PROFESSOR *Melanie Doherty* DEPARTMENT *Graphic Design* DEPARTMENT CHAIR *Michael Vanderbyl* ■ *Project title: "Make Your Own Rosary Kit."* ● *Die Aufgabe war der Entwurf eines eigenen Rosenkranzes.* ▲ *Tâche assignée créer son propre rosaire.*

PAGE 98 IMAGE 302, 303 STUDENT *Elif Memisoglu* SCHOOL *School of Visual Arts* PROGRAM *BFA, Graphic Design, 1996* PROFESSOR *Carin Goldberg* ■ *Fashion promotional piece for Isaac Mizrahi on his "Insex" runway show combining fashion and science.* ● *Promotion für eine Modenschau von Isaac Mizrahi.* ▲ *Kit promotionnel pour un défilé d'Isaac Mizrahi.*

PAGE 98 IMAGE 304 STUDENT *Jim Sewell* SCHOOL *Portfolio Center* PROGRAM *Graphic Design, 1996* PROFESSOR *Hank Richardson*

PAGE 98 IMAGE 305 STUDENT *Terje Vist* SCHOOL *School of Visual Arts* PROGRAM *BFA, Graphic Design* ■ *Self-promotion for a multimedia designer.* ● *Eigenwerbung eines Multimedia-Designers.* ▲ *Publicité autopromotionnelle d'un designer multimédia.*

PAGE 98 IMAGES 306, 307 STUDENT *David Cheung, Jr.* SCHOOL *Kent Institute of Art & Design* PROGRAM *Graphic Design, 3rd year* ■ *Yoga meditation book cover made to be a collector's item.* ● *Umschlag für ein Buch über Yoga, das als Sammelobjekt konzipiert ist.* ▲ *Couverture d'un livre sur le yoga conçue comme un ouvrage de collection.*

PAGE 99 IMAGE 308 STUDENT *Elizabeth Folkerth* SCHOOL *California College of Arts & Crafts, School of Design* PROFESSOR *Michael Vanderbyl* DEPARTMENT *Graphic Design* CHAIR *Leslie Becker* DEAN *Michael Vanderbyl* ■ Project: "Transcendent Moment of Play." ● Der Titel des Projektes: «Der transzendente Augenblick des Spiels.» ▲ Projet intitulé «L'instant sublime du jeu».

PAGE 99 IMAGE 309 STUDENT *Thomas Schopp* SCHOOL *Saginaw Valley State University* PROGRAM *BA, Fine Arts, Minor: Graphic Design* ■ Entry in statewide license plate design contest. ● Entwurf eines Autonummernschildes für einen nationalen Wettbewerb. ▲ Conception de plaques minéralogiques dans le cadre d'un concours national.

PAGE 100 IMAGES 310, 311 STUDENT *Kris DiMatteo* SCHOOL *School of Visual Arts* PROGRAM *BFA, 1996* PROFESSOR *K. O'Callahan* ■ Life size sculpture of Jackson Pollock. ● Eine lebensgrosse Skulptur des Malers Jackson Pollock. ▲ Sculpture grandeur nature de Jackson Pollock.

PAGE 100 IMAGE 312 STUDENT *Shandele Gumucio* SCHOOL *California College of Arts & Crafts, School of Design* PROFESSOR *Michael Vanderbyl* DEPARTMENT *Graphic Design* CHAIR *Leslie Becker* DEAN *Michael Vanderbyl* ■ Project "Under-privileged." ● Titel dieses Projektes «Unterprivilegiert». ▲ Projet intitulé «Under-privileged».

PAGE 101 IMAGE 313, 314 STUDENT *Cherese Rambaldi* SCHOOL *Rhode Island School of Design* PROGRAM *BFA, Senior* PROFESSOR *Aki Nurosi* ■ Purpose: to show proportions visually, not mathematically. ● Darstellung von Proportionen auf visuelle statt auf mathematische Art. ▲ Représentation visuelle (et non mathématique) de proportions.

PAGES 102, 103 IMAGES 315-317 STUDENT *Hans-Heinrich Sures* SCHOOL *Fachhochschule Dortmund* PROGRAM *Graphic Design, 12th semester* PROFESSOR *Dieter Ziegenfeuter*

PAGE 104 IMAGE 318 STUDENT *Andrew Barthelmes* SCHOOL *School of Visual Arts* PROGRAM *BFA, 1996* ■ "Man with Birds." ● «Mann mit Vögeln.» ▲ «L'homme aux oiseaux.»

PAGE 105 IMAGES 319-324 STUDENT *Wolfgang Schmid* SCHOOL *Staatliche Akademie der Bildenden Künste* PROGRAM *Graphic Design, 7th semester* PROFESSOR *Heinz Edelmann* ■ Collages of heads. ● Collagen von Köpfen. ▲ Collages de têtes.

PAGE 105 IMAGE 325 STUDENT *Jason Reed* SCHOOL *Calfornia College of Arts & Crafts, School of Design* PROFESSOR *Dugald Stermer* DEPARTMENT *Illustration* CHAIR *Dugald Stermer* DEAN *Michael Vanderbyl* ■ Illustration entitled "The Truth is Out There." ● Illustration mit dem Titel «Die Wahrheit liegt da draussen.» ▲ Illustration intitulée «La vérité est dehors».

PAGE 106 IMAGE 326 STUDENT *John Hermanowski* SCHOOL *School of Visual Arts* PROGRAM *BFA, 1996* PROFESSOR *M. Mattelson*

PAGE 106 IMAGE 327 STUDENT *Geraldine Pope* SCHOOL *School of Visual Arts* PROGRAM *BFA, 1996* PROFESSOR *J. Chung* ■ Dog on chair. ● Hund auf einem Stuhl. ▲ Chien sur une chaise.

PAGE 106 IMAGE 328 STUDENT *Anne Daunes Dusenberry* SCHOOL *Portfolio Center* PROGRAM *Graphic Design, 1996* PROFESSOR *Hank Richardson*

PAGE 107 IMAGE 329 STUDENT *Aaron Roth* SCHOOL *School of Visual Arts* PROGRAM *BFA, 1996* PROFESSOR *S. Martins*

PAGE 108 IMAGE 330 STUDENT *Gregory Sand* SCHOOL *School of Visual Arts* PROGRAM *BFA, 1996* PROFESSOR *J. Chung* ■ Mother Nature. ● Mutter Natur. ▲ Mère Nature.

PAGE 109 IMAGES 331, 332 STUDENT *Monika Aichele* SCHOOL *Staatliche Akademie der Bildenden Künste* PROGRAM *10th semester, Graphic Design* PROFESSOR *Heinz Edelmann* ■ Illustration on the subject of health. ● Illustration zum Thema Gesundheit. ▲ Illustration sur le thème de la santé.

PAGE 109 IMAGES 333, 334 STUDENT *Frauke Lehn* SCHOOL *Staatliche Akademie der Bildenden Künste* PROGRAM *Graphic Design, 8th semester* PROFESSOR *Heinz Edelmann* ■ Illustration on the subject of "color," e.g. for a printing house. ● Illustration zum Thema Farbe ansich, z.B. für eine Druckerei. ▲ Illustration sur le thème «La couleur en soi», par ex. pour une imprimerie.

PAGE 109 IMAGE 335 STUDENT *Marlis Teem* SCHOOL *Portfolio Center* PROGRAM *Illustration, 1996* PROFESSOR *Gary Weiss*

PAGE 109 IMAGE 336 STUDENT *Vincent Ficarra* SCHOOL *School of Visual Arts* PROGRAM *BFA, 1996* ■ Woman with kite. ● Frau mit Drachen. ▲ Femme au cerf-volant.

PAGE 110 IMAGE 337 STUDENT *Gennaro Capasso* SCHOOL *School of Visual Arts* PROGRAM *BFA, 1996* PROFESSOR *M. Mattelson* ■ Dog in Armor. ● Hund in Rüstung. ▲ Chien en armure.

PAGE 110 IMAGE 338 STUDENT *Jules Hsu* SCHOOL *School of Visual Arts* PROGRAM *BFA, 1996* ■ Hillary Clinton. ● Porträt von Hillary Clinton. ▲ Portrait d'Hillary Clinton.

PAGE 110 IMAGE 339 STUDENT *Donald Sipley* SCHOOL *School of Visual Arts* PROGRAM *BFA, 1996* ■ Girl with Blue Birds. ● Mädchen mit blauen Vögeln. ▲ La fillette aux oiseaux bleus.

PAGE 110 IMAGE 340 STUDENT *Kwan Kim* SCHOOL *School of Visual Arts* PROGRAM *BFA, 1996* PROFESSOR *R. Goldstrom* ■ Mouse and computer. ● Maus und Computer. ▲ Souris et ordinateur.

PAGE 111 IMAGE 341 STUDENT *Joseph Stawicki* SCHOOL *University of Connecticut* PROGRAM *BFA, 1996* PROFESSOR *John Fawcett* ■ Illustration for the cover of MOBY DICK, done in black and white on scratchboard. ● Illustration, Schabkarton in Schwarzweiss, für den Umschlag des Buches «Moby Dick». ▲ Illustration pour la couverture de Moby Dick. réalisée en noir et blanc sur carte grattage.

PAGE 112 IMAGE 342 STUDENT *Brian Donnelly* SCHOOL *School of Visual Arts* PROGRAM *BFA, 1996* PROFESSOR *M. Mattelson* ■ "Snake in Window." ● Schlange im Fenster. ▲ Serpent dans la fenêtre.

PAGE 113 IMAGES 343-346 STUDENT *Thomas Fuchs* SCHOOL *Staatliche Akademie der Bildenden Künste* PROGRAM *Graphic Design* PROFESSOR *Heinz Edelmann* ■ Illustrations for "The Hunting of the Snark" by Lewis Carroll. ● Ilustrationen zu "The Hunting of the Snark", ein Gedicht von Lewis Carroll. ▲ Illustrations de La Chasse au snark, un poème de Lewis Carroll.

PAGE 114 IMAGE 347 STUDENT *Sean Greene* SCHOOL *School of Visual Arts* PROGRAM *BFA, 1996*

PAGE 114 IMAGE 348 STUDENT *Jack Paccione* SCHOOL *School of Visual Arts* PROGRAM *BFA, 1996*

PAGE 114 IMAGE 349 STUDENT *Sacha Twaros* SCHOOL *School of Visual Arts* PROGRAM *BFA, 1996* PROFESSOR *F. Jetter* ■ Piranhas in black-and-white. ● Piranhas in Schwarzweiss. ▲ Piranhas en noir et blanc.

PAGE 114 IMAGE 350 STUDENT *Sylvia Neuner* SCHOOL *Staatliche Akademie der Bildenden Künste* PROGRAM *Graphic Design, 6th semester* PROFESSOR *Heinz Edelmann* ■ Illustrations on the subject of "Eating". Technique acrylic and colored pencil. ● Illustrationen zum Thema «Essen». Technik Acryl und Buntstift. ▲ Illustrations sur le thème «Manger». Techniques utilisées peinture acrylique et crayons de couleur.

PAGE 115 IMAGE 351 STUDENT *Renata Lauterbach* SCHOOL *School of Visual Arts* PROGRAM *BFA, 1996*

PAGE 115 IMAGE 352 STUDENT *Isabel Klett* SCHOOL *Staatliche Akademie der Bildenden Künste* PROGRAM *Graphic Design, 8th semester* PROFESSOR *Heinz Edelmann* ■ Illustration for a poem entitled "The Dragon's Alphabet" by Dieter Brembs. ● Illustration zu dem Gedicht «Das Drachen-Abeceh» von Dieter Brembs. ▲ Illustration du poème de Dieter Brembs L'abécédaire du Dragon.

PAGE 116 IMAGE 353 STUDENT *Jason Reed* SCHOOL *Calfornia College of Arts & Crafts* PROFESSOR *Dugald Stermer* DEPARTMENT *Illustration* CHAIR *Dugald Stermer,* DEAN *Michael Vanderbyl* ■ Illustration entitled "Shadow Dancer." ● Illustration mit dem Titel «Schattentänzer». ▲ Illustration intitulée «Shadow Dancer».

PAGE 117 IMAGE 354 STUDENT *Neil O'Brien* SCHOOL *School of Visual Arts* PROGRAM *BFA, 1996*

PAGE 117 IMAGE 355 STUDENT *Jay Juch* SCHOOL *School of Visual Arts* PROGRAM *BFA, 1996* PROFESSOR *J. Chung* ■ *Flying lion.* ● *Fliegender Löwe.* ▲ *Lion volant.*

PAGE 117 IMAGE 356 STUDENT *Elizabeth V. Witmer* SCHOOL *School of Visual Arts* PROGRAM *BFA, 1996* PROFESSOR *S. Martins* ■ *"Birdcage."* ● *Vogelkäfig.* ▲ *Cage à oiseaux.*

PAGE 117 IMAGE 357 STUDENT *James P. Mandella* SCHOOL *School of Visual Arts* PROGRAM *BFA, 1996* PROFESSOR *S. Martins* ■ *"Alien dog."* ● *Ausserirdischer Hund.* ▲ *Chien extra-terrestre.*

PAGE 118 IMAGE 358, 359 STUDENT *Amie Walter* SCHOOL *Oregon State University* PROGRAM *BFA, Senior* PROFESSOR *David Hardesty*

PAGE 118 IMAGE 360 STUDENT *Steve Clifton* SCHOOL *Portfolio Center* PROGRAM *Graphic Design, 1996* PROFESSOR *Hank Richardson*

PAGE 119 IMAGE 361 STUDENT *Danniel Gaidula* SCHOOL *University of Missouri at Columbia* PROGRAM *BFA, Art & Graphic Design* PROFESSOR *Andrea Witczak* ■ *Self-promotion.* ● *Eigenwerbung.* ▲ *Publicité autopromotionnelle.*

PAGE 120 IMAGES 362, 363 STUDENT *So Takahashi* SCHOOL *School of Visual Arts* PROGRAM *BFA, 1996* PROFESSOR *Chris Austopchuck* CLASS *Portfolio* ■ *Corporate identity for a store called "Evolution" which sells bugs, fossils and all other things concerned with nature.* ● *C.I.-Design für einen Laden mit dem Namen «Evolution», der Käfer, Fossilien und Ähnliches verkauft.* ▲ *Identité visuelle pour le magasin d'insectes et de fossiles «Evolution».*

PAGE 120 IMAGE 364 STUDENT *Michelle Gray* SCHOOL *University of Missouri at Columbia* PROGRAM *BA, Journalism* ■ *Design of an identity system for a traveling exhibit about American architect Louis Sullivan.* ● *C.I.-Programm für eine Wanderausstellung über die Arbeit und Ideen des amerikanischen Architekten Louis Sullivan.* ▲ *Programme d'identité visuelle pour une exposition itinérante consacrée au travail et aux idées de l'architecte américain Louis Sullivan.*

PAGE 120 IMAGE 365 STUDENT *Machiko Matsufuji* SCHOOL *School of Visual Arts* PROGRAM *BFA, Graphic Design, 1996* PROFESSOR *Christopher Austopchuk* ■ *Design done for Anna Sui.* ● *Design für Anna Sui.* ▲ *Design pour Anna Sui.*

PAGE 121 IMAGE 366 STUDENT *Yael Daphna* SCHOOL *School of Visual Arts* PROGRAM *BFA* CLASS *Type & Design* PROFESSOR *Henrietta Condak* ■ *Menu and identity for Zen Palate, a vegetarian Japanese restaurant* ● *Speisekarte und Erscheinungsbild für Zen Palate, ein vegetarisches japanisches Restaurant.* ▲ *Carte et identité visuelle pour le restaurant japonais Zen Palate, spécialisé dans la cuisine végétarienne.*

PAGE 121 IMAGE 367 STUDENT *Sha-Mayne Chan* SCHOOL *School of Visual Arts* PROGRAM *Graphic Design, 1996* PROFESSOR *Carin Goldberg* ■ *Logo and stationery for the Variety Arts Theatre.* ● *Logo und Briefpapier für das Variety Arts Theatre.* ▲ *Logo et papier à lettres pour le Variety Arts Theatre.*

PAGE 121 IMAGE 368 STUDENT *Hubie Le* SCHOOL *Portfolio Center* PROGRAM *Graphic Design, 1996* PROFESSOR *Hank Richardson*

PAGE 121 IMAGE 369 STUDENT *Sharon Wyatt* SCHOOL *University of Delaware* PROGRAM *BS, Visual Communications, 1996* PROFESSOR *Martha Carothers* ■ *Letterhead, logo and business card design for a photographer.* ● *Briefpapier, Logo und Visitenkarte für einen Photographen.* ▲ *Papier à lettres, logo et carte de visite pour un photographe.*

PAGE 121 IMAGE 370 STUDENT *Terje Vist* SCHOOL *School of Visual Arts* PROGRAM *BFA Graphic Design* ■ *Stationery system for an art bookstore in Soho.* ● *Briefpapier für einen Kunstbuchladen in Soho.* ▲ *Papier à lettres pour une librairie d'ouvrages d'art de Soho.*

PAGE 121 IMAGE 371 STUDENT *Andrew Reed* SCHOOL *Oregon State University* PROGRAM *BFA, Senior* PROFESSOR *David Hardesty*

PAGE 122 IMAGES 372, 373 STUDENT *Clemens Hilger* SCHOOL *Fachhochschule Mainz* PROGRAM *Communication Design, 1994* PROFESSOR *Olaf Leu.* ■ *Stationery system completed as part of thesis work.* ● *Teil einer Diplomarbeit: Briefpapier und Signet*

für Grafische Greim. ▲ *Eléments d'un travail de diplôme: papier à lettres et marque de la maison Grafische Greim.*

PAGE 122 IMAGES 374, 375 STUDENT *Peter Vajda* SCHOOL *Hungarian Academy of Fine Arts* PROGRAM *3rd year, Graphic Design* ■ *Design of a logo.* ● *Gestaltung eines Logos.* ▲ *Création d'un logo.*

PAGE 123 IMAGES 376, 377 STUDENT *Andrew Reed* SCHOOL *Oregon State University* PROGRAM *BFA, Senior* PROFESSOR *David Hardesty*

PAGE 124 IMAGE 378 STUDENT *Kristin Standiford* SCHOOL *University of Oregon* PROGRAM *BFA, Senior* PROFESSOR *Robin Kilgore*

PAGE 124 IMAGES 379 STUDENT *Marshall Faircloth* SCHOOL *Portfolio Center* PROGRAM *Graphic Design, 1996* PROFESSOR *Hank Richardson*

PAGE 124 IMAGE 380 STUDENT *Beatriz Peiro* SCHOOL *Escuela Artes y Oficios* PROFESSOR *Gonzalo Mora*

PAGE 124 IMAGE 381 STUDENT *Marshall Faircloth* SCHOOL *Portfolio Center* PROGRAM *Graphic Design, 1996* PROFESSOR *Hank Richardson*

PAGE 125, IMAGE 382 STUDENT *Carsten Bolk* SCHOOL *Universität GH Essen* CLASS *Kommunikations Design, 10th semester*

PAGE 125 IMAGE 383 STUDENT *Shelae Howden* SCHOOL *Western Washington Unversity* PROGRAM *BA, Graphic Design, Senior* PROFESSOR *Kent Smith* ■ *Three-dimensional translation of a two-dimensional logo.* ● *Dreidimensionale Interpretation eines zweidimensionalen Logos.* ▲ *Interprétation tridimensionnelle d'un logo en deux dimensions.*

PAGE 126 IMAGE 384 STUDENT *Hubie Le* SCHOOL *Portfolio Center* PROGRAM *Graphic Design, 1996* PROFESSOR *Hank Richardson*

PAGE 126 IMAGE 385 STUDENT *Gratia Gast* SCHOOL *Portfolio Center* PROGRAM *Graphic Design, 1996* PROFESSOR *Hank Richardson*

PAGE 126 IMAGE 386 STUDENT *Lisa Critchfield* SCHOOL *University of Utah* PROGRAM *BFA Graphic Design, 1997* PROFESSOR *Mac Magleby* CLASS *Visual Communication* ■ *Animal logo.* ● *Tier-Logo.* ▲ *Logo animal.*

PAGE 126 IMAGE 387 STUDENT *Sharon Slaughter* SCHOOL *Portfolio Center* PROGRAM *Graphic Design, 1996* PROFESSOR *Hank Richardson*

PAGE 126 IMAGE 388 STUDENT *Gratia Gast* SCHOOL *Portfolio Center* PROGRAM *Graphic Design, 1996* PROFESSORS *Hank Richardson, Ted Fabella*

PAGE 127 IMAGE 389 STUDENT *Marshall Faircloth* SCHOOL *Portfolio Center* PROGRAM *Graphic Design, 1996* PROFESSOR *Hank Richardson*

PAGE 127 IMAGES 390, 391 STUDENT *Senta Brockschmidt* SCHOOL *Fachhochschule Mainz* PROGRAM *Communication Design, 4th year* PROFESSOR *Olaf Leu* ■ *Corporate identity for the printing, publishing and media service "Konkordia."* ● *C.I. Design für einen Druck, Verlags- und Mediendienst Konkordia.* ▲ *Identité visuelle pour le prestataire de services Konkordia travaillant dans l'impression, l'édition et les médias.*

PAGE 127 IMAGE 392 STUDENT *Taiwai D. Yun* SCHOOL *Bernard Baruch College* PROGRAM *Graphic Communication, Senior* CLASS *Corporate Design* PROFESSOR *Virginia Smith* ■ *This icon was developed to identify a new department for a college Web page.* ● *Diese Ikone wurde für die Web-Seite eines neuen College-Studienganges entworfen.* ▲ *Icone conçue pour une Page Web présentant un nouveau programme d'études.*

PAGE 128 IMAGES 393-397 STUDENT *Karin Kaiser* SCHOOL *Staatliches Akademie der Bildenden Künste* PROGRAM *Graphic Design,* PROFESSOR *Hans-Georg Pospischil* ■ *Logos for different columns of a magazine.* ● *Logos für verschiedene Rubriken einer Zeitschrift Archiv, Zeitraffer, Neuland, Service, Leseprobe.* ▲ *Logos réalisés pour les différentes rubriques d'un magazine archives, en bref, découvertes, services, littérature.*

PAGE 128 IMAGE 398 STUDENT *Reli Cardosa* SCHOOL *Escola Artística e Profissional Arvore*

PAGE 128 IMAGE 399 STUDENT *Victor Rocha* SCHOOL *Escola Artistica e Profissional Arvore* PROGRAM *Graphic Design* PROFESSOR *Carla Cadete*

PAGE 128 IMAGE 400 STUDENT *Cathy Else* SCHOOL *Western Washington University* DEGREE *BA Graphic Design, Senior* PROFESSOR *Elsi Vassdal-Ellis* CLASS *Graphic Design II*

PAGE 128, IMAGE 401 STUDENT *João Pedro Guerreiro* SCHOOL *Escola Artistica e Profissional Arvore* PROFESSOR *Carla Cadete*

PAGE 128 IMAGE 402 STUDENT *Cristina Monteiro* SCHOOL *Escola Artistica e Profissional Arvore* PROGRAM *Graphic Design, 3rd level* PROFESSOR *Carla Cadete*

PAGE 128 IMAGES 403-412 STUDENT *Rui Cardoso* SCHOOL *Escola Artistica e Profissional Arvore* PROGRAM *Graphic Design, 3rd level* PROFESSOR *Carla Cadete* ■ *Icons for different disciplines of the Olympic Games.* ● *Symbole für verschiedene Disziplinen der Olympischen Spiele.* ▲ *Pictogrammes pour différentes disciplines des Jeux olympiques.*

PAGE 129 IMAGE 413 STUDENT *Peter Vajda* SCHOOL *Hungarian Academy of Fine Arts* PROGRAM *3rd year, Graphic Design*

PAGE 129 IMAGE 414 STUDENT *Peter Vajda* SCHOOL *Hungarian Academy of Fine Arts* PROGRAM *3rd year, Graphic Design* ■ *Logo created for Open Society of Archives at the Central European University.* ● *Logo für die Bibliothek einer Universität.* ▲ *Logo réalisé pour les archives d'une université.*

PAGE 130 IMAGE 415 STUDENT *Russ Sokoloff* SCHOOL *School of Visual Arts* PROGRAM *BFA, 1996* ■ *Menu design for a Cajun and seafood restaurant.* ● *Speisekarte für ein Fischrestaurant.* ▲ *Carte d'un restaurant de spécialités de poisson.*

PAGES 130, 131 IMAGES 416-419 STUDENT *Yael Daphna* SCHOOL *School of Visual Arts* PROGRAM *BFA, Sophomore* PROFESSOR *Henrietta Condak* CLASS *Type & Design.* ■ *Menu and identity for Zen Palate, a vegetarian Japanese restaurant.* ● *Speisekarte und Erscheinungsbild für Zen Palate, ein vegetarisches japanisches Restaurant.* ▲ *Carte et identité visuelle pour le restaurant japonais Zen Palate, spécialisé dans la cuisine végétarienne.*

PAGE 131 IMAGES 420, 421 STUDENT *Daniel Conlan* SCHOOL *California State University at Fullerton* PROGRAM *BFA Graphic Design, Senior* PROFESSOR *Steven Abeyta*

PAGE 132 IMAGE 422 STUDENT *P.M. Reeves* SCHOOL *Baylor University* PROGRAM *Graphic Design, 1996* PROFESSOR *Mark Moran* ■ *Graphic for local TV program called "Live at 5."* ● *Graphik für ein lokales TV-Programm mit dem Titel "Live at 5".* ▲ *Projet graphique pour le programme d'une chaîne régionale intitulé «Live at 5».*

PAGES 132, 133 IMAGES 423-429 STUDENT *Nicola Wimmershoff* SCHOOL *Fachhochschule Mainz* PROGRAM *Communication Design, 1994* PROFESSOR *Jörg Osterspey* ■ *Corporate design for Photoshop software completed as part of thesis.* ● *C.I.-Design für Photoshop-Software als Teil einer Diplomarbeit.* ▲ *Identité visuelle pour le logiciel Photoshop. Travail de diplôme.*

PAGE 134 IMAGES 430-435 STUDENT *So Takahashi* SCHOOL *School of Visual Arts* PROGRAM *BFA, 1996* PROFESSOR *Chris Austopchuck* CLASS *Portfolio* ■ *Three CD package designs.* ● *Verpackungen für drei CDs.* ▲ *Packagings de CD.*

PAGE 135 IMAGE 436 STUDENT *Aki Inoue* SCHOOL *School of Visual Arts* PROGRAM *BFA, Senior* PROFESSOR *Jeffrey Keyton* ■ *David Bowie special CD package design.* ● *Verpackung für eine "David Bowie Special"-CD.* ▲ *Boîtier créé pour la compilation «David Bowie Special».*

PAGE 136 IMAGE 437 STUDENT *Suzanne Ach* SCHOOL *School of Visual Arts* PROGRAM *BFA, Graphic Design, Senior* PROFESSOR *Carin Goldberg* ■ *CD package targeting adolescent market and with all profits going to the World Wildlife Fund.* ● *Verpackung für eine CD, deren Verkaufserlös an den World Wildlife Fund geht.* ▲ *Packaging de CD ciblant les adolescents. L'intégralité des recettes sera reversée au WWF.*

PAGE 136 IMAGE 438 STUDENT *Aki Inoue* SCHOOL *School of Visual Arts* PROGRAM *BFA, Senior* PROFESSOR *Jeffrey Keyton* ■ *Madonna "Pain," single CD design.* ● *Gestaltung einer CD von Madonna.* ▲ *Design d'un CD de Madonna.*

PAGE 136 IMAGE 439 STUDENT *Roswitha Rodrigues* SCHOOL *School of Visual Arts* PROGRAM *BFA, Junior* PROFESSOR *Stacy Drummond* ■ *Special edition packaging of CD featuring music from the motion picture "The Mask."* ● *Verpackung einer 'Special Edition CD' mit Musik aus dem Film "The Mask".* ▲ *Packaging d'un CD de la musique du film The Mask, édition limitée.*

PAGE 137 IMAGE 440 STUDENT *Rachel Meltzer* SCHOOL *School of Visual Arts* PROGRAM *BFA, 1997* PROFESSOR *Henrietta Condak* ■ *CD cover and booklet.* ● *CD-Hülle und Broschüre.* ▲ *Boîtier et livret de CD.*

PAGE 137 IMAGE 441 STUDENT *Cherese Rambaldi* SCHOOL *Rhode Island School of Design* PROGRAM *BFA, Senior* PROFESSOR *Hammett Nurosi* CLASS *Design Applications* ■ *Package and booklet design for a special edition collectors' CD.* ● *Gestaltung der Hülle und Broschüre für eine Special Edition CD für Sammler.* ▲ *Réalisation du boîtier et du livret d'un CD en série limitée.*

PAGE 137 IMAGE 442 STUDENTS *Markus Fischer, Pit Lederle (Discodoener)* SCHOOL *Staatliche Akademie der Bildenden Künste* PROGRAM *4th semester, Graphic Design* PROFESSOR *Günter Jacki* ■ *Flyer for a disco.* ● *Flyer für eine Diskothek.* ▲ *Flyer pour une discothèque.*

PAGE 138 IMAGE 443 STUDENT *Gratia Gast* SCHOOL *Portfolio Center* PROGRAM *Graphic Design, 1996* PROFESSOR *Hank Richardson*

PAGE 139 IMAGE 444 STUDENT *Kyota Gima* SCHOOL *Academy of Art College* PROGRAM *BFA, 1995-1996* PROFESSOR *Michael Osborne* CLASS *Package Design 4* ■ *Assignment: expand product line and design packaging for Nike.* ● *Aufgabe Erweiterung der Produktpalette und Verpackungsgestaltung für Nike.* ▲ *Sujet élargissement de la gamme de produits et design de packagings pour Nike.*

PAGE 140 IMAGE 445 STUDENT *Tara Benyei* SCHOOL *Academy of Art College* PROGRAM *BFA, 1995-1996* PROFESSOR *Ray Honda* CLASS *Package Design 3* ■ *Packaging for Speed Racer lager.* ● *Verpackungsgestaltung für ein Bier.* ▲ *Packaging réalisé pour une bière.*

PAGE 140 IMAGE 446 STUDENT *William Pflipsen* SCHOOL *Moorhead State University* PROGRAM *BFA, Graphic Design, 1997* PROFESSOR *Phil Mouseau* CLASS *Graphics 400* ■ *Assignment: develop a unique package design for an imported beer.* ● *Verpackungsgestaltung für ein Importbier.* ▲ *Packaging réalisé pour une bière d'importation*

PAGE 140 IMAGE 447 STUDENT *Yvette Tam* SCHOOL *Academy of Art College* PROGRAM *BFA, 1995-1996* PROFESSOR *Philippe Becker* CLASS *Package Design* ■ *Redesign of packaging for Tsing-Tao beer.* ● *Überarbeitung der Verpackung von Tsing-Tao-Bier.* ▲ *Packaging revisité pour la bière Tsing-Tao.*

PAGE 141 IMAGE 448 STUDENT *Brian Uber* SCHOOL *Western Washington University* PROGRAM *Graphic Design, 1996* PROFESSOR *Kent Smith* CLASS *3-Dimensional Graphic Design.* ■ *Cola label and six-pack design for Autocola.* ● *Gestaltung des Cola-Etiketts und eines Six-Packs.* ▲ *Design de l'étiquette d'une boisson au cola et d'un pack de six bouteilles.*

PAGE 142 IMAGES 449-451 STUDENT *Muriel Häfeli* SCHOOL *Schule für Gestaltung Zürich* PROGRAM *Graphic Design, 4th semester* PROFESSOR *Daniel Volkart* ■ *Wine labels for a wine store called La Bottiglia.* ● *Weinetiketten für La Bottiglia, einen Weinladen.* ▲ *Etiquettes créées pour La Bottiglia, un négociant en vins.*

PAGE 143 IMAGES 452-454 STUDENT *Miriam Meyer-Jung* SCHOOL *Fachhochschule Mainz* PROGRAM *Communication Design* PROFESSOR *Jörg Osterspey* ■ *Corporate identity design for a winery completed as part of thesis project.* ● *C.I. Design für ein Weingut als Teil der Diplomarbeit.* ▲ *Identité visuelle pour un négociant en vins, réalisée dans le cadre d'un travail de diplôme.*

PAGE 143 IMAGE 455 STUDENT *Keiko Rost* SCHOOL *Academy of Art College* PROGRAM *BFA, 1995-1996* PROFESSOR *Darryl Reed* CLASS *Package Design 3* ■ *Packaging design for a sake.* ● *Verpackung für einen Sake.* ▲ *Packaging pour un saké.*

PAGE 143 IMAGE 456 STUDENT *Elif Memisoglu* SCHOOL *School of Visual Arts* PROGRAM *BFA, Graphic Design, 1996* PROFESSOR *Carin Goldberg* CLASS *Portfolio* ■ *Wine label.* ● *Weinetikett.* ▲ *Etiquette de vin.*

PAGE 143 IMAGE 457 STUDENT *Lian Ng* SCHOOL *Academy of Art College* PROGRAM *Bachelor of Fine Arts, 1995-1996* PROFESSOR *Marc Tedeschi* CLASS *Corporate Systems* ■ *Packaging for Beringer wine.* ● *Packungsgestaltung für einen Wein.* ▲ *Packaging pour les vins Beringer.*

PAGE 144 IMAGE 458 STUDENT *Tone Stromberg* SCHOOL *Academy of Art College* PROGRAM *BFA, 1995-1996* PROFESSOR *Darryl Reed* CLASS *Package Design 3* ■ *Redesign of existing packaging for a vodka company.* ● *Überarbeitung der vorhandenen Verpackungen eines Wodka-Herstellers.* ▲ *Toilettage des packagings d'une marque de vodka.*

PAGE 144 IMAGE 459 STUDENT *Coco Qui* SCHOOL *Academy of Art College* PROGRAM *BFA, 1995-1996* PROFESSOR *Darryl Reed* CLASS *Package Design 3* ■ *Re-design existing packaging for vodka company.* ● *Überarbeitung der vorhandenen Verpackungen eines Wodka-Herstellers.* ▲ *Toilettage des packagings d'une marque de vodka.*

PAGE 144 IMAGE 460 STUDENT *Caroline Fernandes* SCHOOL *Academy of Art College* PROGRAM *BFA, 1995-1996*

PAGE 144 IMAGE 461 STUDENT *Rebecca Sepulveda* SCHOOL *Academy of Art College* PROGRAM *BFA, 1995-1996* PROFESSOR *Darryl Reed* ■ *Redesign of packaging and logo for existing cognac company.* ● *Überarbeitung der Verpackung und des Logos für einen Cognac.* ▲ *Nouveaux packaging et logo pour un cognac.*

PAGE 145 IMAGE 462 STUDENT *Derek Sussner* SCHOOL *University of Minnesota* PROGRAM *Design Communications, 1996* PROFESSOR *Jake Jacobson* CLASS *Package Design* ■ *Assignment: to create an identity and label design for a new whiskey brand.* ● *Gestaltung des Markenauftritts und des Etiketts für eine neue Whiskey-Marke.* ▲ *Création d'une identité visuelle et d'une étiquette pour une nouvelle marque de whisky.*

PAGE 146 IMAGE 463 STUDENT *Hubie Le* SCHOOL *Portfolio Center* PROGRAM *Graphic Design, 1996* PROFESSOR *Hank Richardson*

PAGE 147 IMAGE 464 STUDENT *Melissa Laux* SCHOOL *Academy of Art College* PROGRAM *BFA, 1995-1996* PROFESSOR *Ray Honda* CLASS *Package Design 3.* ■ *Packaging for MAC cosmetics* ● *Verpackung für MAC-Kosmetik.* ▲ *Packaging pour la ligne de cosmétiques MAC.*

PAGE 148 IMAGE 465 STUDENT *Charlie Beale* SCHOOL *Somerset College of Art + Technology* PROGRAM *2nd year, Graphic Design* PROFESSOR *Jack Gardner* ■ *Cosmetics packaging.* ● *Packungsgestaltung für Kosmetik.* ▲ *Packaging pour une ligne de cosmétiques.*

PAGE 149 IMAGE 466 STUDENT *Aya Kotake* SCHOOL *Academy of Art College* PROGRAM *BFA, 1995-1996* PROFESSOR *Darryl Reed* CLASS *Package Design 3* ■ *Armani Urbano identity and package design for ficticious store.* ● *C.I.-Design und Verpackungen für einen fiktiven Laden Armani Urbano.* ▲ *Identité visuelle et packaging pour le magasin fictif Armani Urbano.*

PAGE 150 IMAGE 467 STUDENT *Amanda Billings* SCHOOL *Kent Institute of Art & Design* PROGRAM *BA, Communication Media*

PAGE 151 IMAGE 468-470 STUDENT *So Takahashi* SCHOOL *School of Visual Arts* PROGRAM *BFA, 1996* PROFESSOR *Chris Austopchuck* ■ *Vitamin 12 essential box set.* ● *Gestaltung eines Verpackungssets für ein Vitaminpräparat.* ▲ *Création d'une famille d'emballages pour un complexe vitaminé.*

PAGE 152 IMAGE 471 STUDENT *Patricia Giblet* SCHOOL *Somerset College of Art + Technology, School of Communication & Performing Arts* PROGRAM *2nd year, Graphic Design* PROFESSOR *Jack Gardner* ■ *Packaging for pet foods.* ● *Verpackung für Tiernahrung.* ▲ *Packaging pour de la nourriture pour animaux.*

PAGE 153 IMAGE 472 STUDENT *Emily Selwood* SCHOOL *Somerset College of Art + Technology, School of Communication & Performing Arts* PROGRAM *Graphic design 2nd year* PROFESSOR *Jack Gardner* ■ *Packaging for pet foods.* ● *Verpackung für Tiernahrung.* ▲ *Packaging pour de la nourriture pour animaux.*

PAGE 154 IMAGE 473 STUDENT *Kamajayawaty Hartawan* SCHOOL *Academy of Art College* PROGRAM *BFA, 1995-1996* PROFESSOR *Michael Osborne* CLASS *Package Design 4*

PAGE 155 IMAGE 474 STUDENT *Sarah Tutt* SCHOOL *Somerset College of Art +Technology, School of Communication & Performing Arts* PROGRAM *Graphic Design, 2nd year* PROFESSOR *Jack Gardner.* ■ *Pet food packaging.* ● *Verpackung für Tiernahrung.* ▲ *Packaging pour de la nourriture pour animaux.*

PAGE 155 IMAGE 475 STUDENT *Kelly Godfrey* SCHOOL *Somerset College of Art +Technology, School of Communication & Performing Arts* PROGRAM *Graphic Design, 2nd year* PROFESSOR *Jack Gardner* ■ *Pet food packaging.* ● *Verpackung für Tiernahrung.* ▲ *Packaging pour de la nourriture pour animaux.*

PAGE 155 IMAGE 476 STUDENT *Tara Benyei* SCHOOL *Academy of Art College* PROGRAM *BFA, 1995-1996* PROFESSOR *Philippe Becker* ■ *Packaging for Perugina coffee.* ● *Verpackung für einen Kaffee.* ▲ *Packaging pour un café.*

PAGE 154 IMAGE 477 STUDENT *Kamajayawaty Hartawan* SCHOOL *Academy of Art College* PROGRAM *BFA, 1995-1996* PROFESSOR *Michael Osborne* CLASS *Package Design* ■ *Assignment: develop a unique packaging design and name.* ● *Die AufgabeEntwurf einer einzigartigen Verpackung und des Markennamens.* ▲ *Sujet création d'un packaging et d'un nom de marque.*

PAGE 154 IMAGE 478 STUDENT *Michael Tompert* SCHOOL *Academy of Art College* PROGRAM *BFA, 1995-1996* PROFESSOR *Ray Honda* CLASS *Package Design 3* ■ *Brand identity and packaging for Reese, a seafood company.* ● *Gestaltung der Marke und der Verpackung für eine Firma, die mit Meeresfrüchten handelt.* ▲ *Création d'une identité et design de packaging pour une société spécialisée dans les fruits de mer.*

PAGE 154 IMAGE 479 STUDENT *Keiko Rost* SCHOOL *Academy of Art College* PROGRAM *BFA, 1995-1996* PROFESSOR *Package Design 3* ■ *Redesign of packaging for Schilling spices.* ● *Überarbeitung einer Verpackung für Schilling-Gewürze.* ▲ *Rajeunissement du packaging des épices Schilling.*

PAGE 156 IMAGE 480 STUDENT *Christine Darnell* SCHOOL *Academy of Art College* PROGRAM *BFA, 1995-1996*

PAGE 157 IMAGE 481 STUDENT *Anja Wille* SCHOOL *Fachhochschule Mainz* PROGRAM *10th semester* PROFESSOR *Olaf Leu* ■ *New packaging design for a brand of chocolate.* ● *Neugestaltung der Verpackung für ein Schokoladenprodukt.* ▲ *Nouveau packaging pour une marque de chocolat.*

PAGE 157 IMAGE 482 STUDENT *Sarah Sirlin, Mary Beth Joyce* SCHOOL *Portfolio Center* PROGRAM *Graphic Design, 1996* PROFESSOR *Hank Richardson*

PAGE 158 IMAGE 483 STUDENT *Michele Stepanek* SCHOOL *Academy of Art College* PROGRAM *BFA, 1995-1996* PROFESSOR *Ralph Colonna* ■ *Packaging for Knipex.* ● *Verpackung für Knipex.* ▲ *Packaging réalisé pour Knipex.*

PAGE 159 IMAGE 484 STUDENT *Elif Memisoglu* SCHOOL *School of Visual Arts* PROGRAM *BFA, Graphic Design, 1996* PROFESSOR *Carin Goldberg* ■ *Simple, inexpensive packaging for clothespins.* ● *Graphisch ansprechende Verpackung für ein ganz alltägliches Produkt: Wäscheklammern.* ▲ *Packaging simple pour un produit usuel les pinces à linge.*

PAGE 159 IMAGE 485 STUDENT *Suzanne Ach* SCHOOL *School of Visual Arts* PROGRAM *BFA, Graphic Design* PROFESSOR *Carin Goldberg* ■ *This packaging design provides the consumer a fun way of testing the size of a bolt.* ● *Diese Verpackung ermöglicht dem Verbraucher, die Grösse einer Schraube auf witzige Art zu testen.* ▲ *Packaging permettant au consommateur de tester la taille d'une vis de façon ludique.*

PAGE 159 IMAGE 486 STUDENT *Iris Lee* SCHOOL *School of Visual Arts* PROFESSOR *Chris Austopchuk* ■ *Light bulb package design.* ● *Verpackung für Glühbirnen.* ▲ *Packaging pour des ampoules électriques.*

PAGE 160 IMAGE 487 STUDENT *Thomas Melanson* SCHOOL *Brigham Young University* PROGRAM *BFA, Senior* PROFESSOR *Adrian Pulfer* CLASS *Packaging* ■ *This redesign of packaging for tie-dye products emphasizes the chemical nature of fabric dying.* ● *Überarbeitung der Verpackung für Textilfärbemittel, wobei der chemische Prozess des Färbens das Thema lieferte.* ▲ *Nouveau packaging pour des teintures textiles. Thème le processus chimique de teinture.*

PAGE 160 IMAGE 488 STUDENT *Jennifer Matic* SCHOOL *Rhode Island School of Design* PROGRAM *BFA, Graphic Design, Senior* PROFESSOR *Aki Nurosi, Sarah Flynn* CLASSES *Package Design, Intro to Jewelry and Light Metals* ■ *Packaging and product design.* ● *Verpackungs- und Produkt-Design.* ▲ *Packaging et design de produit.*

PAGE 161 IMAGE 489 STUDENT *Marshall Faircloth* SCHOOL *Portfolio Center* PROGRAM *Graphic Design, 1996* PROFESSOR *Hank Richardson*

PAGE 161 IMAGE 490 STUDENT *Jim Hackleman* SCHOOL *Savannah College of Art And Design* PROGRAM *MFA* PROFESSOR *Colin Gearing* CLASS *Package Design* ■ *Assignment: develop and introduce an imaginary line of car care products.* ● *Entwicklung und Einführung einer Linie von Autopflegemitteln.* ▲ *Design et lancement d'une ligne fictive de produits d'entretien pour voitures.*

PAGE 161 IMAGES 491, 492 STUDENT *Ingo Ditges* SCHOOL *Staatliche Akademie der Bildenden Künste* PROGRAM *6th Semester* PROFESSOR *Hans-Georg Pospischil* ■ *Packaging of a poster on the subject of "Art and Commerce" (perspectives of photography).* ● *Verpackung für ein Plakat zum Thema «Kunst und Kommerz», (Perspektiven in der Photographie).* ▲ *Packaging d'une affiche sur le thème «Art et Commerce» (perspectives de la photographie).*

PAGE 162, 163 IMAGE 493, 494 STUDENT *Emy Kat* SCHOOL *Brooks Institute of Photography* CLASS *Lighting People* PROFESSOR *Paul Mayer, Bob Smith*

PAGE 164 IMAGE 495 STUDENT *Ashley Rush* SCHOOL *Art Institute of Atlanta* PROGRAM *Associates, 1996* PROFESSOR *Phillip Becker* CLASS *Portfolio* ■ *Product shot for portfolio.* ● *Produktaufnahme für die Arbeitsmappe.* ▲ *Prise de vue pour un portfolio.*

PAGE 165 IMAGE 496 STUDENT *Anthony Sullivan* SCHOOL *Long Island University* PROGRAM *Sophomore* PROFESSOR *Carol Heubner* ■ *Photo taken for color photo final exam.* ● *Photo für die Abschlussprüfung in Farbphotographie.* ▲ *Photo réalisée pour l'examen final de photographie couleur.*

PAGE 165 IMAGE 497 STUDENT *Marjorie Torres* SCHOOL *Portfolio Center* PROGRAM *Photography, 1996* PROFESSOR *Ray Ellis*

PAGE 166 IMAGE 498 STUDENT *Emy Kat* SCHOOL *Brooks Institute of Photography*

PAGE 167 IMAGE 499 STUDENT *Samuel D. Morris* SCHOOL *Art Institute of Atlanta* PROGRAM *Associate in Photography, 1996* PROFESSOR *Phillip Becker* CLASS *Portrait Portfolio*

PAGE 168 IMAGE 500 STUDENT *Kristen VanCott* SCHOOL *Portfolio Center* PROGRAM *Photography, 1996* PROFESSOR *Ray Ellis*

PAGE 169 IMAGE 501 STUDENT *Samuel D. Morris* SCHOOL *Art Institute of Atlanta* PROGRAM *Associate in Photography, 1996* PROFESSOR *Phillip Becker*

PAGE 169 IMAGES 502, 503 STUDENT *Kiet T. Le* SCHOOL *Orange Coast College* PROGRAM *Certificate in Photography, 1996* CLASS *Commercial Photography* PROFESSOR *Rick Steadry* ■ *Outdoor shots taken for Black Crow Clothing Company for an editorial piece on fashion in a sports magazine. Taken with an R267 camera, a 127mm lens, and T-max 100 film.* ● *Aussenaufnahmen für einen Modebeitrag in einem Sportmagazin. Die vorgestellten Kleider sind von der Crow Clothing Company.* ▲ *Prises de vue en extérieur pour les pages mode d'un magazine de sport. Les vêtements présentés sont signés Crow Clothing Company.*

PAGE 170 IMAGE 504 STUDENT *Theresa Cioppa* SCHOOL *Art Institute of Atlanta* PROGRAM *Associates, 1995* PROFESSOR *Phillip Becker* CLASS *Studio Ii* ■ *Class assignment on glassware.* ● *Ein Gruppenprojekt, bei dem es um Glasgegenstände ging.* ▲ *Projet de groupe sur des objets en verre.*

PAGE 170 IMAGE 505 STUDENT *John Stormont* SCHOOL *Portfolio Center* PROGRAM *Photography, 1996* PROFESSOR *Ray Ellis*

PAGE 170 IMAGE 506 STUDENT *Donsoo Choi* SCHOOL *Portfolio Center* PROGRAM *Photography, 1996* PROFESSOR *Ray Ellis*

PAGE 170 IMAGE 507 STUDENT *Kristen VanCott* SCHOOL *Portfolio Center* PROGRAM *Photography, 1996* PROFESSOR *Ray Ellis*

PAGE 171 IMAGE 508 STUDENT *Andreas Pawlitzki, Carsten Bolk* SCHOOL *Universität Gesamthochschule Essen* PROGRAM *Communication Design, 10th semester* PROFESSOR *Inge Osswald* ■ *Architectural photography showing the Abteiberg Museum in Mönchengladbach, Germany.* ● *Architekturaufnahme des Abteiberg-Museums in Mönchengladbach.* ▲ *Photo d'architecture du Musée Abteiberg de Mönchengladbach, Allemagne.*

PAGE 172 IMAGE 509 STUDENT *Alex Chu Yew Tien* SCHOOL *Rocky Mountain College of Art and Design* ■ *"Drive carefully. Unless you are made of steel." This poster targets youth and promotes safe driving.* ● *«Fahr vorsichtig. Es sei denn, Du bist aus Stahl.» Ein an Jugendliche gerichtetes Plakat, bei dem es um vernünftiges Fahrverhalten geht.* ▲ *«Vas-y mollo! A moins que tu ne sois en acier.» Affiche invitant les jeunes à conduire prudemment.*

PAGE 172 IMAGE 510 STUDENT *Lloyd Rodrigues* SCHOOL *School of Visual Arts* PROGRAM *BFA, 1996* ■ *This poster combines the Lord's prayer with the pledge of allegiance.* ● *Das Plakat verbindet das Vaterunser mit der Aufforderung zur Treue und will damit zum Gespräch anregen.* ▲ *Affiche combinant le Notre Père et le serment d'allégeance, dont le propos était de fournir un thème de discussion.*

PAGE 173 IMAGE 511 STUDENT *Kedar Gore* SCHOOL *The Art Institute of Atlanta* PROGRAM *Associates, 1996* PROFESSOR *Phillip Becker* ■ *Poster design for portfolio category requirement.* ● *Plakat als Beispiel seiner Art, für die Arbeitsmappe des Studenten.* ▲ *Affiche d'un étudiant créée pour son portfolio.*

PAGES 174, 175 IMAGES 512-517 STUDENT *Vera Hoffmann* SCHOOL *Fachhochschule Dortmund* PROGRAM *Graphic Design* PROFESSOR *Dieter Ziegenfeuter*

PAGE 176 IMAGES 518-520 STUDENT *Heather Snyder* SCHOOL *Rhode Island School of Design* PROGRAM *BFA Graphic Design, 1996* PROFESSOR *Aki Nurosi* CLASS *Color and Application* ■ *This series of four posters in homage to the designer Bradbury Thompson demonstrates the power of color as a design tool.* ● *Die Serie von vier Plakaten ist eine Hommage an den verstorbenen Graphiker Bradbury Thompson. Thema ist die Kraft der Farbe als Gestaltungsmittel.* ▲ *Hommage à Bradbury Thompson. Série de quatre affiches illustrant l'impact de la couleur comme instrument de design.*

PAGE 177 IMAGE 521 STUDENT *Ramona Sparks* SCHOOL *University of Missouri at Columbia* PROGRAM *BA in Art with Graphic Design emphasis, Senior* PROFESSOR *Andrea Witczak* CLASS *Graphic Design IV* ■ *Identity system for museum exhibition of architect Michael Graves* ● *Gestaltung des gesamten C.I.-Programms für eine Ausstellung, die dem Architekten Michael Graves gewidmet ist.* ▲ *Programme d'identité visuelle pour l'exposition d'un musée consacrée à l'architecte Michael Graves.*

PAGE 178 IMAGE 522 STUDENT *Robert Karyshyn* SCHOOL *Ringling School of Art and Design* CLASS *Graphic Design 2* PROFESSOR *Douglas Higgins* ■ *"The origin of creativity. Everything I know I taught myself."* ● *«Der Ursprung der Kreativität. Alles, was ich weiss, habe ich mir selbst beigebracht.»* ▲ *«L'origine de la créativité. Tout ce que je sais, je l'ai appris moi-même.»*

PAGE 179 IMAGE 523 STUDENT *Chihiro Hosoe* SCHOOL *Rhode Island School of Design* PROGRAM *BFA* PROFESSOR *Malcolm Grear* CLASS *Form and Structure* ■ *This poster is a culmination of the student's work for a class on form and structure.* ● *Plakat eines Studenten für die Klasse Form und Struktur.* ▲ *Affiche réalisée par un étudiant dans le cadre du cours Forme et Structure.*

PAGE 179 IMAGE 524 STUDENT *Jonathan Weis* SCHOOL *Oregon State University* PROGRAM *BFA, Senior* PROFESSOR *Andrea Marks*

PAGE 179 IMAGE 525 STUDENT *Chihiro Hosoe* SCHOOL *Rhode Island School of Design* PROGRAM *BFA* PROFESSOR *Nancy Skolos* ■ *Announcement of a new illustration font.* ● *Ankündigung einer neuen, der Illustration dienenden Schrift.* ▲ *Présentation d'une nouvelle police de caractères destinée à l'illustration.*

PAGE 179 IMAGE 526 STUDENT *Connie Hwang* SCHOOL *University of Washington* PROGRAM *MFA, Graphic Design* PROFESSOR/ART DIRECTOR *Chris Ozubko*

PAGE 180 IMAGE 527 STUDENT *Dominic Trautvetter* SCHOOL *Fachhochschule Dortmund* PROGRAM *Graphic Design, 12th semester* ■ *Poster for a photo contest and symposium.* ● *Plakat für einen photographischen Wettbewerb und ein Symposium.* ▲ *Affiche pour un symposium et un concours photo.*

PAGE 181 IMAGE 528 STUDENT *Aya Kotake* SCHOOL *Academy of Art College* PROGRAM *BFA, 1995-1996* PROFESSOR *Paul Tsang* CLASS *Graphic Design 3* ■ *Poster for a professional baseball park.* ● *Plakat für einen professionellen Baseball-Platz.* ▲ *Affiche pour un terrain de base-ball professionnel.*

PAGE 182 IMAGE 529 STUDENT *Sang-Joon Lee* SCHOOL *School of Visual Arts* PROGRAM *BFA, 1996* PROFESSOR *Alex Knowlton* ■ *This poster pokes fun at the proliferation of telemarketing calls from the local and national telephone services.* ● *Das Plakat macht sich über die Ausbreitung der Tele-Marketing-Aktionen von lokalen und nationalen Telephondiensten lustig.* ▲ *Affiche tournant en dérision les opérations de télémarketing de services téléphoniques régionaux et nationaux.*

PAGE 183 IMAGE 530 STUDENT *Regina Krutoy* SCHOOL *School of Visual Arts* PROGRAM *BA, Senior* PROFESSOR *Henrietta Condak* CLASS *Graphic Design* ■ *A series of posters based on AIDS awareness.* ● *Eine Plakatserie zum Thema AIDS.* ▲ *Série d'affiches sur le sida.*

PAGE 184 IMAGES 531-533 STUDENT *Meridith McRae* SCHOOL *University of Utah* PROGRAM *BFA, 1996* PROFESSOR *McRay Magleby* CLASS *Graphic Illustration* ■ *Three-piece poster illustration series promoting a musical event.* ● *Dreiteiliges Plakat für eine Musikveranstaltung.* ▲ *Triptyque pour un événement musical.*

PAGE 185 IMAGE 534 STUDENT *Luke Chueh* SCHOOL *California Polytechnic* PROGRAM *B.S., Senior* PROFESSOR *Mary LaPorte* ■ *Design for the Envision 22 student poster contest sponsored by the ADAC.* ● *Plakat für einen Studenten-Plakatwettbewerb.* ▲ *Affiche réalisée dans le cadre d'un concours d'étudiants.*

PAGE 186 IMAGE 535 STUDENTS *Christina Bazzini, Cheryl Bernett, Michael Bondoc, Andria Davis, Mare Dianora, Brad Eisenstein, Abigail Fein, Karen Gergely, Rich McGuigan, Amy Meomartino, Matt Nuzzi, Melanie Petrin, Ashley Pigford, Glenn Stevens, Dave Wasserman, Sharon Wyatt* SCHOOL *University of Delaware* PROGRAM *B.S. Visual Communications, 1996* PROFESSORS *Martha Carothers, Ray Nichols* ■ *Poster promoting year-end exhibition of student design work.* ● *Plakat für eine Ausstellung von Studentenarbeiten.* ▲ *Affiche réalisée dans le cadre d'un concours d'étudiants.*

PAGE 186 IMAGE 536 STUDENT *Amie Walter* SCHOOL *Oregon State University* PROGRAM *BFA, Senior* PROFESSOR *Stephen Chovanec*

PAGE 187 IMAGE 537 STUDENT *Sha-Mayne Chan* SCHOOL *School of Visual Arts* PROGRAM *Graphic Design, 1996* PROFESSOR *Carin Goldberg* ■ *Poster for three one-act comedies titled "Death Defying Acts" at the Variety Arts Theatre.* ● *Plakat für die Aufführung von drei einaktigen Komödien am Variety Arts Theatre.* ▲ *Affiche pour une comédie en un seul acte du Variety Arts Theatre.*

PAGE 187 IMAGE 538 STUDENT *Barbara Melluso* SCHOOL *School of Visual Arts* PROGRAM *BFA Graphic Design, 1996* PROFESSOR *Carin Goldberg* ■ *Assignment: Design a poster to promote a play.* ● *Plakat für eine Theateraufführung.* ▲ *Affiche de théâtre.*

PAGE 188 IMAGE 539-541 STUDENT *Terje Vist* SCHOOL *School of Visual Arts* PROGRAM *BFA Graphic Design, Senior* PROFESSOR ■ *Alan Parker trilogy.* ● *Ankündigung einer Alan-Parker-Trilogie.* ▲ *Présentation d'une trilogie d'Alan Parker.*

PAGE 189 IMAGE 542 STUDENT *Ingrid Forbord* SCHOOL *School of Visual Arts* PROGRAM *BFA, Senior* PROFESSOR *Carin Goldberg* ■ *Theater poster.* ● *Theaterplakat.* ▲ *Affiche de théâtre.*

PAGES 190, 191 IMAGES 543, 544 STUDENTS *Hans-Heinrich Sures, Ingo Eulen* SCHOOL *Fachhochschule Dortmund* PROGRAM *Graphic Design* ■ *Poster for a symposium on the film formats "Scope" and "Super 34."* ● *Plakat für ein Symposium über die Filmformate "Scope" und "Super 35".* ▲ *Affiche pour un symposium sur les films en cinémascope et en super 35.*

PAGE 192 IMAGE 545 STUDENTS *Hizam Haron, Joan Raspo* SCHOOL *California College of Arts & Crafts, School of Design* PROFESSOR *Jennifer Morla* CHAIR *Leslie Becker*

DEAN *Michael Vanderbyl* ■ *Project: poster for the Gay and Lesbian Alliance Against Defamation (GLAAD).* ● *Plakat für die Vereinigung der Lesbierinnen und Homosexuellen gegen Defamierung.* ▲ *Affiche pour l'Association contre la discrimination des lesbiennes et des homosexuels.*

PAGE 192 IMAGE 546 STUDENTS *Shandele Gumucio, Mary Hayano* SCHOOL *California College of Arts & Crafts* CLASS *Graphic Design 4* PROFESSOR *Lisa Levin* DEAN *Michael Vanderbyl* ■ *Greyhound Protection League poster.* ● *Plakat für eine Vereinigung zum Schutz des Windhundes.* ▲ *Affiche pour l'Association de protection des lévriers.*

PAGE 192 IMAGE 547 STUDENT *Lisa Salonen* SCHOOL *Cranbrook Academy of Art* PROGRAM *MFA, 1997* PROFESSOR *Katherine McCoy*

PAGE 192 IMAGE 548 STUDENT *Johnny Pak Chung-Lai* SCHOOL *Tsing Yi Technical College* PROGRAM *Graphic Design* ■ *"AIDS not only kills men." One of a series of posters designed to generate public awareness of AIDS in Hong Kong. The student was responsible for concept generation, photography, copy, artwork and layout.* ● *«AIDS tötet nicht nur Männer.» Eines aus einer Serie von Plakaten, die über AIDS in Hongkong informiert. Der Student war für Konzept, Photographie, Text, Graphik und Layout verantwortlich.* ▲ *«Le sida ne tue pas que les hommes.» Affiche extraite d'une série sur le sida à Hongkong. L'étudiant était responsable du concept, de la photographie, de la rédaction, du graphisme et du layout.*

PAGE 193 IMAGE 549 STUDENT *Gaby Brink* SCHOOL *California College of Arts & Crafts* PROGRAM *Graphic Design* PROFESSOR *Lucille Tenazas* DEAN *Michael Vanderbyl*

PAGE 194 IMAGES 550, 551 STUDENT *Christie Lau* SCHOOL *California College of Arts and Crafts* CLASS *Industrial Design 4* PROFESSORS *Yves Behár, Max Yoshimoto* CHAIR *Steven Skov Holt* ■ *The projector is designed for the home environment. A friendly and whimsical gesture is captured by the abstract human form. Images can be viewed by either plugging in the digital camera or inserting the photo CD.* ● *Der Projektor ist für den Privatgebrauch bestimmt. Die abstrakte menschliche Gestalt gibt ihm ein skurriles, liebenswertes Aussehen. Die Bilder können entweder durch Anschliessen der digitalen Kamera oder durch Einschieben der Photo-CD angeschaut werden.* ▲ *Projecteur à usage domestique. Le personnage abstrait lui confère un côté étrange et sympathique. Les images peuvent être visionnées avec un caméscope numérique ou en insérant le CD photo.*

PAGE 194 IMAGE 552 STUDENT *Peter Vajda* SCHOOL *Hungarian Academy of Fine Arts* PROGRAM *3rd year, Graphic Design*

PAGE 195 IMAGE 553 STUDENT *James Morrison* SCHOOL *Parsons School of Design* PROGRAM *BFA Product Design, 1996* PROFESSOR *Laurene Leon, Constantin Boym* CLASS *Product Design 2* ■ *Shoe designed for post-sports relaxation for Reebok design competition.* ● *Im Rahmen eines Designwettbewerbs von Reebok entworfener Schuh, der beim Entspannen nach dem Sport getragen werden soll.* ▲ *Créée dans le cadre d'un concours Reebok, cette chaussure de relaxation est destinée à être portée après l'effort sportif.*

PAGE 195 IMAGE 554 STUDENT *Insun Yun* SCHOOL *Parsons School of Design* PROGRAM *BFA Product Design, 1996* PROFESSORS *Laurene Leon, Constantin Boym* CLASS *Product Design 2* ■ *Inflatable shoe designed for post-sports relaxation for Reebok design competition.* ● *Für einen Reebok-Designwettbewerb entworfener, luftgefederter Schuh, der beim Entspannen nach dem Sport getragen werden soll.* ▲ *Créée dans le cadre d'un concours Reebok, cette chaussure de relaxation montée sur coussins d'air est destinée à être portée après l'effort sportif.*

PAGE 195 IMAGES 555, 556 STUDENT *Jennifer Gibbs* SCHOOL *Parsons School of Design* PROGRAM *BFA Furniture Design, 1996* PROFESSOR *Constantin Boym* ■ *Product name: The Backpack Chair.* ● *Name des Produktes: Rucksack-Stuhl.* ▲ *Chaise «sac à dos».*

PAGE 195 IMAGE 557 STUDENT *David Simon* SCHOOL *California College of Arts and Crafts* PROFESSORS *Stephen Peart, David Peschel,* CHAIR *Steven Skov Holt* ■ *Product name: Shoe Storage Object. Photography by Steven Moeder.* ● *«Objekt für die Unterbringung von Schuhen», photographiert von Steven Moeder.* ▲ *Meuble à chaussures, photo de Steven Moeder.*

PAGE 195 IMAGE 558 STUDENT *Jessica Corr* SCHOOL *Parsons School of Design* PROGRAM *BFA Furniture Design, 1996* PROFESSOR *Constantin Boym* ■ *Movable occasional tables.* ● *Mobile Beisetztische.* ▲ *Dessertes.*

PAGE 195 IMAGE 559 STUDENT *Sandra Hesla* SCHOOL *California College of Arts and Crafts* PROFESSORS *Stephen Peart, David Peschel* CLASS *Industrial Design 5* CHAIR *Steven Skov Holt*

PAGE 195 IMAGE 560 STUDENT *Helene Ige* SCHOOL *Parsons School of Design* PROGRAM *BFA Furniture Design* PROFESSOR *Constantin Boym* ■ *Multi-purpose outdoor furnishings. Product name: The Everlasting Gobb Stopper.* ● *Mehrzweckgerät für draussen.* ▲ *Mobilier d'extérieur multifonctionnel.*

PAGE 196 IMAGE 561 STUDENT *Steve Penny* SCHOOL *California College of Arts and Crafts* PROGRAM *Industrial Design*

PAGE 196 IMAGE 562 STUDENT *Joshua W. Ferguson* SCHOOL *California College of Arts and Crafts* PROFESSORS *Kevin Elston, Pam Carpenter* ■ *Assignment: design and build a chair predominantly out of wood. Project title: Waterfall Chair. Materials: maple/alder 9-ply, dowels. Design Strategy: The student wished to create a feeling of rivers and waterfalls through fluidity of form. To achieve this, he used the strength and aesthetic properties of 9-ply to create the flex-back design, with each vertical member of the chair reflecting the tendency of rivers to wash toward the outside of the bend, while the overall effect is that of water pouring down, pooling in the seat area, and spilling off in all directions.* ● *Gestaltung eines Stuhls, der vorwiegend aus Holz bestehen sollte. Name Wasserfall-Stuhl, Material Ahorn/Erle (9 Schichten) und Dübel. Die Form sollte das Gefühl von fliessendem Wasser vermitteln. Das herabstürzende Wasser sammelt sich zu einem Becken (im Sitz) und strömt dann in alle Richtungen.* ▲ *Design d'une chaise dont le principal matériau devait être le bois. Nom du projet chaise «chute d'eau». Matériaux érable, aulne (9 couches) et fenton. La forme devait suggérer le ruissellement de l'eau, les eaux de la cascade s'écoulant pour former un bassin (l'assise) avant de rejaillir dans toutes les directions*

PAGE 196 IMAGES 563, 564 STUDENT *Deklah Polansky* SCHOOL *School of Visual Arts* PROGRAM *BFA, 1996* PROFESSOR *Stacy Dramond* ■ *Self-portrait in the form of a chair.* ● *Selbstporträt in Form eines Stuhls.* ▲ *Autoportrait en forme de chaise.*

PAGE 196 IMAGES 565, 566 STUDENT *Nurit Haddas* SCHOOL *School of Visual Arts* PROGRAM *BFA, 1996* PROFESSOR *Stacy Dramond* ■ *Self-portrait in the form of a chair.* ● *Selbstporträt in Form eines Stuhls.* ▲ *Autoportrait en forme de chaise.*

PAGE 197 IMAGE 567 STUDENTS *Christopher Smith, Mark Bolick, Anna Lisa Sigmarsdottir, Beth Forbes* SCHOOL *California College of Arts and Crafts* PROFESSORS *Fred Bould, Craig Janik* CLASS *Industrial Design 2* CHAIR *Steven Skov Holt* ■ *Group meeting center.* ● *Besprechungszentrum.* ▲ *Centre de rencontres*

PAGE 197 IMAGE 568 STUDENTS *Jonah Becker, Robert Hudson, Jason Poyner, Jake Rivas* SCHOOL *California College of Arts and Crafts* PROFESSOR *Craig Janik, Fred Bould* CLASS *Industrial Design 2* CHAIR *Steven Skov Holt* ■ *Project name: Modular Conference Table.* ● *Aus Elementen konzipierter Konferenztisch.* ▲ *Table de conférences modulaire.*

PAGE 198 IMAGE 569 STUDENT *Bard Gronvold* SCHOOL *California College of Arts and Crafts* PROFESSORS *Yves Behar, Max Yoshimoto* CLASS *Industrial Design 4* CHAIR *Steven Skov Holt* ■ *Product: Snowboard.* ● *Produkt: Snowboard-Gerät.* ▲ *Accessoire de snowboard.*

PAGE 198 IMAGE 570 STUDENT *Jonah Becker* SCHOOL *California College of Arts and Crafts* PROFESSORS *Craig Janik, Fred Bould* CLASS *Industrial Design 2* CHAIR *Steven Skov Holt* ■ *Product: Camping flashlight.* ● *Produkt Camping-Taschenlampe.* ▲ *Lampe de poche.*

PAGE 198 IMAGE 571 STUDENT *Marshall Faircloth* SCHOOL *Portfolio Center* PROGRAM *Graphic Design, 1996* PROFESSOR *Hank Richardson*

PAGE 198 IMAGE 572 STUDENT *Ragnhild Haugum* SCHOOL *Parsons School of Design* PROGRAM *BFA Product Design, 1996* PROFESSORS *Laurene Leon, Constantin Boym* CLASS *Product Design 2* ■ *Recreational seat called "Snow Siesta" for tired skiers created for Reebok design competition.* ● *Für einen Reebok-Design-Wettbewerb entworfener Sitz für müde Skiläufer.* ▲ *Sièges de relaxation pour skieurs moulus, créé dans le cadre d'un concours Reebok.*

PAGE 199 IMAGE 573 STUDENT *Richard Unger* SCHOOL *Universität Gesamthochschule Essen* PROGRAM *Communication Design, 12th semester* PROFESSOR *Vilim Vasata* ■ *Watch incorporating an "E" for the city of Essen. Each hour for one second the hands of the watch form the Essen logo. The watch will be launched in June 1997.* ● *Gestaltung einer Armbanduhr im Auftrag der Stadt Essen, unter Einbeziehung des «E» im Logo der Stadt Essen. Jede Stunde ergibt sich eine Sekunde lang eine Zeigerkonstellation, die das Logo der Stadt zeigt. Die Uhr kommt im Juni 1997 auf den Markt.* ▲ *Création d'une montre-bracelet pour la ville d'Essen intégrant le «E» de son logotype. Toutes les heures, les aiguilles de la montre forment, l'espace d'une seconde, le logo de la ville. Cette montre sera commercialisée en juin 1997.*

PAGE 199 IMAGE 574 STUDENT *Christie Lau* SCHOOL *California College of Arts and Crafts* PROFESSORS *Yves Behar, Max Yoshimoto* CLASS *Industrial Design 4* CHAIR *Steven Skov Holt* ■ *Product: in-line skater's helmet, photography by Steven Moeder.* ● *Helm für Inline-Skater, photographiert von Steven Moeder* ▲ *Casque pour inline-skaters, photo de Steven Moeder*

PAGE 200 IMAGE 575 STUDENT *Jannie Lai* SCHOOL *California College of Arts and Crafts* PROFESSOR *Stephen Peart, David Peschel* CLASS *Industrial Design 5* CHAIR *Steven Skov Holt* ■ *Product: Soft Children's Computer, photography by Doug Sandberg.* ● *Weicher Computer für Kinder, photographiert von Doug Sandberg.* ▲ *Ordinateur pour enfants, photo de Doug Sandberg.*

PAGE 200 IMAGE 576 STUDENT *Terral Cochran* SCHOOL *University of Utah* PROGRAM *BFA, Senior* PROFESSOR *Raymond C. Morales* ■ *Senior project: combine a clock with an activity or an occupation.* ● *Bei diesem Projekt für Studenten der oberen Semester ging es darum, eine Uhr mit einer Aktivität oder Beschäftigung zu verbinden.* ▲ *Projet d'étudiants en fin d'études créer une montre en rapport avec une activité ou un passe-temps.*

PAGE 201 IMAGES 577, 578 STUDENT *Andy Randazzo* SCHOOL *School of Visual Arts* PROGRAM *Graphic Design, Senior 1996* PROFESSOR *Kevin O'Callaghan* ■ *A useless object transformed and given new life.* ● *Thema Verwandlung und neues Leben für ein vormals nutzlos gewordenes Objekt.* ▲ *Thème transformer un objet inutile et lui donner vie.*

PAGE 201 IMAGES 579, 580 STUDENT *Jonah Becker, Ivy Leung, Jenya Pechenaya, Jake Rivas, Brian Yumae* SCHOOL *California College of Arts and Crafts* PROFESSOR *Tim Sheiner, Albert Lum* CLASS *Product Design 2* CHAIR *Steven Skov Holt* ■ *Product: personal digital assistant.* ● *Das Produkt: ein persönlicher, digitaler Assistent.* ▲ *Le produit: un assistant personnel numérique.*

PAGE 201 IMAGES 581, 582 STUDENT *Celia Landegger* SCHOOL *School of Visual Arts* PROGRAM *BFA, Graphic Design, 1996* PROFESSOR *Kevin O'Callaghan* ■ *Assignment: Given a Yugo automobile as a point of departure, create a life for it other than the one that was originally intended.* ● *Ausgangsprodukt der Aufgabe war ein altes, jugoslawisches Auto, das einen anderen Verwendungszweck erhalten sollte.* ▲ *La tâche assignée consistait à transformer un vieux tacot yougoslave (Yugo) et à lui attribuer une nouvelle fonction.*

PAGE 201 IMAGES 583, 584 STUDENT *Jason Pamental* SCHOOL *Rhode Island College* PROGRAM *BFA Graphic Design, 1998* PROFESSOR *Nancy Evans* CLASS *Graphic Design 2* ■ *Create six matchboxes with a related theme.* ● *Sechs Zündholzschachteln mit zusammenhängenden Themen.* ▲ *Création de six boîtes d'allumettes déclinées sur un même thème.*

PAGE 202 IMAGE 585 STUDENT *Aya Kotake* SCHOOL *Academy of Art College* PROGRAM *BFA, 1995-1996* PROFESSOR *Julia Brown* ■ *Supercuts annual report.* ● *Jahresbericht.* ▲ *Rapport annuel.*

PAGE 202 IMAGE 586 STUDENT *Connie Hwang* SCHOOL *University of Washington* PROGRAM *MFA* PROFESSOR/ART DIRECTOR *Chris Ozubko*

PAGE 203 IMAGE 587 STUDENT *Andy Randazzo* SCHOOL *School of Visual Arts* PROGRAM *Graphic Design, Senior 1996* PROFESSOR *Alexander Knowlton* ■ *Poster design for the Isamu Noguchi Garden Museum located in Queens, New York.* ● *Plakat für das Isamu Noguchi-Gartenmuseum in Queens, New York.* ▲ *Affiche pour le Musée du jardin Isamu Noguchi dans le Queens, New York.*

PAGE 204 IMAGES 588, 590 STUDENT *Machiko Matsufuji* SCHOOL *School of Visual Arts* PROGRAM *BFA, Graphic Design, 1996* PROFESSOR *Christopher Austopchuk* ■ *Design for fashion designer Anna Sui.* ● *Design für Anna Sui.* ▲ *Design pour Anna Sui.*

PAGE 204 IMAGE 589 STUDENT *Joanne Rounds* SCHOOL *Al Collins Graphic Design School* PROGRAM *AA, 1996* PROFESSOR *Debra Cook* CLASS *3-D Design*

PAGE 205 IMAGE 591 STUDENT *Péter Vajda* SCHOOL *Hungarian Academy of Fine Arts* PROGRAM *Graphic Design, 3rd year*

PAGE 206 IMAGE 592 STUDENT *Marshall Faircloth* SCHOOL *Portfolio Center* PROGRAM *Graphic Design, 1996* PROFESSOR *Hank Richardson*

PAGE 206 IMAGE 593 STUDENT *Terje Vist* SCHOOL *School of Visual Arts* PROGRAM *BFA, Graphic Design* ■ *Stamp commemorating Lennart Nilson who photographed life before birth.* ● *Briefmarke zu Ehren von Lennart Nilson, der einen Weg fand, pränatales Leben zu photographieren.* ▲ *Timbre créé en hommage à Lennart Nilson, photographe de la vie avant la naissance.*

PAGE 206 IMAGE 594 STUDENT *Sindy Stol Birkfeld* SCHOOL *Kent Institute of Art and Design*

PAGE 207 IMAGE 595 STUDENT *Alex Chu Yew Tien* SCHOOL *Rocky Mountain College of Art* ■ *This design promotes environmental awareness.* ● *Das Thema Förderung des Umweltbewusstseins.* ▲ *Sujet sensibiliser l'opinion à adopter un comportement écologique*

PAGE 208 IMAGE 596 STUDENT *Carmina Silvia* SCHOOL *Istituto Europeo di Design* PROGRAM *Graphic Design, 2nd year*

PAGE 209 IMAGES 597-599 STUDENT *Pablo Arroyo* SCHOOL *Istituto Europeo di Design* PROGRAM *Graphic Design, 2nd year* ■ *Class assignment, consisting of twenty-seven letters, ten numbers and five signs, the size of each letter being 6.5 cm high and 5 cm wide.* ● *Gruppenprojekt, bei dem es insgesamt um 27 Buchstaben, 10 Nummern und 5 Zeichen ging, wobei jeder Buchstabe 6,5cm hoch und 5cm breit war.* ▲ *Projet de groupe portant sur 27 lettres, 10 chiffres et 5 signes. Chaque caractère devait mesurer 6,5 cm de haut pour une largeur de 5 cm.*

PAGE 210 IMAGES 600-602 STUDENT *Sabine Kreuzer* SCHOOL *Fachhochschule Mainz* PROGRAM *Graduate thesis work, Typography* PROFESSOR *Eberhard Peil* ■ *Development of headline-type numbers on the basis of constructive, geometric forms.* ● *Eine von drei verschiedenen Headline-Schriften und Nummern im Rahmen einer Diplomarbeit. Als Gestaltungselement dienten konstruktive, geometrische Formen.* ▲ *Création des éléments typographiques d'une headline pour un travail de diplôme, sur la base de formes constructives et géométriques.*

LAST PAGE STUDENT *Nurit Haddas* SCHOOL *School of Visual Arts* PROGRAM *BFA, 1996* PROFESSOR *Stacy Dramond* ■ *Self-portrait in the form of a chair.* ● *Selbstporträt in Form eines Stuhls.* ▲ *Autoportrait en forme de chaise.*

INDEX

VERZEICHNISSE

INDEX

. . . .

S T U D E N T S · S T U D E N T E N · E T U D I A N T S

. . . .

. . . .

S T U D E N T S · S T U D E N T E N · E T U D I A N T S

. . . .

. . . .

S C H O O L S · U N I V E R S I T Ä T E N · U N I V E R S I T É S

. . . .